For Melanie and the little "F"

TREVOR **MERRIDEN**

Rollercoaster

The Turbulent Life and Times of **Vodafone** and **Chris Gent**

CAPSTONE

First published 2003 by

Capstone Publishing Ltd (A John Wiley & Sons Co.)
8 Newtec Place
Magdalen Road
Oxford OX4 1RE
United Kingdom
http://www.capstoneideas.com

British Library Cataloguing in Publication Data
A CIP catalogue record for this book is available from the British Library

ISBN 1-84112-431-1

Typeset by
Forewords, 109 Oxford Road, Cowley, Oxford

Printed and bound by
T.J. International Ltd, Padstow, Cornwall

This book is printed on acid-free paper

Substantial discounts on bulk quantities of Capstone books are available to corporations, professional associations and other organizations. For details contact Capstone Publishing by telephone (+44-1865-798623), fax (+44-1865-240941), or email (info@wiley-capstone.co.uk).

Contents

Preface

I have always been fascinated by Chris Gent and Vodafone. Along with others, I watched in awe as Gent pulled off an astonishing series of acquisitions, including that of Mannesmann, the largest hostile takeover in corporate history, as he transformed a UK mobile phone company into a global powerhouse. Then I watched in considerably less awe as I saw the Vodafone share price halve, and then halve again over the following two years, accompanied by a steady barrage of media criticism over the size of Gent's pay packet.

When I was approached in early 2002 by Mark Allin of Wiley-Capstone Publishing to write an independent book about Vodafone I was delighted at the chance of learning more. And during the course of my research I discovered that the rollercoaster that Vodafone has been riding during the six years of Gent's tenure (and before) was far more complex and compelling than I had realized.

Most of all I learned how quickly – and how undeservedly – reputations of personalities and the companies they run can be made and lost. Gent was picked as *Forbes* Global Businessman of the year for 1999. Three years later Vodafone was drawing comparisons with basket case companies such Marconi and WorldCom because of its massive losses. The earlier accolade was premature in the extreme. Gent had completed staggering acquisitions in 1999 and the early part of 2000, but had not yet had an opportunity to prove that they could work. The later brickbat was even more absurd, as any cursory examination of the numbers will reveal. What this book does try to show above all, therefore, is the rollercoaster ride of Chris Gent and Vodafone outside of the context of every-day media sensationalism.

The book is divided as follows. The introduction starts near the "end" of the Gent era. After six years of massive ups and downs, Gent hit back at critics with an excellent set of results in November 2002. He seemed to be back in fashion but, as we now know, within a few weeks he was to announce his departure. How did we get to this point?

The answer lies in the chapters that follow. "Here Come the Buccaneers" looks at the early days of Gent and Vodafone. "Shy Sam and Curious Klaus" charts Gent's progress as he snaps up AirTouch in the US and is provoked by the antics of Klaus Esser of Mannesmann.

The next two chapters focus on the battle for Mannesmann. "The Impossible Dream" examines how Gent fought to get his takeover bid off the ground in the face of unfavourable odds. "Blood and Betrayal" looks at the heat of the battle between Vodafone and Mannesmann executives.

The next section examines what life at the top of the corporate rollercoaster was like for Gent, and for Vodafone. "Red Devils and Prancing Horses" shows how Vodafone's new found status allowed it to pay for the global sponsorship of Manchester United and Ferrari. "Trouble in Vodaville" reveals how the arrogance of corporate power nearly led Vodafone to score a disastrously costly own-goal in its home town of Newbury.

The next part of the book looks at the scary downward rollercoaster ride endured by the company after the bubble in technology stocks finally burst. "From Powerhouse to Penny Share" explains why Vodafone stock ended up at only a quarter of its all time high. "The Trouble with Money" looks at the massive problems caused to the reputations of both Vodafone and Gent by the controversy surrounding his remuneration.

The final two chapters show how Gent and Vodafone hit back. In "Back in Fashion" we return to the opening point of the book, with Gent back at his best and delivering success. Finally, "Now You See Him, Now You Don't" explains why he decided to leave, what his legacy is and what his successor will bring.

One housekeeping point: I have deliberately referred to Sir Christopher Gent as Chris Gent throughout the text. This is not a mark of disrespect. Rather, I wanted to refer to him in the manner used by most of those to whom I spoke.

I would like to thank all of the many interviewees for this book. Some only agreed to speak on the condition of anonymity and these wishes have been respected. Thanks also to all at Wiley-Capstone, especially Mark Allin, John Moseley, Grace O'Byrne and Kate Santon for their expert support in the writing of this book. Friends and colleagues took the time either to review draft chapters or help in other ways. In no particular order they are: Dominic Mills, editorial director of Haymarket Business Publications and *Campaign* magazine; David Prosser of the *Daily Express*; Sarah Bridge of the *Mail on Sunday*; Andrew Davidson of the *Sunday Times*; Stefan Stern of *Human Resources* and *Management Today* magazines; and Francesca Cunningham of *Business Voice*. Thanks also to Tim Brown of Vodafone for his prompt responses to questions of fact.

Most of all, however, thank you to my wife Melanie who gave me marvellous love and support over the period in which this book has been written. It's taken far too long, so thanks above all for your patience.

Trevor Merriden
March 31, 2003
St Albans

Introduction

Back in Fashion – November 12, 2002

It's a day of drizzle in London. The press filters into the Savoy Hotel's Riverside entrance as the clock shows ten minutes to midday. Vodafone's half-year trading figures have just been announced and the mood of its executives is highly excitable. The mobile phone giant has just announced a 40% leap in profits.

Just outside the Savoy's Ballroom, where a press conference is due to take place, Thomas Geitner, the German responsible for the group's products and services, is looking relaxed. His role today will not be on the podium – "It's my day off from that," he grins. But you sense that these are a set of figures that the Geitner wouldn't mind presenting. A tall man with wire glasses in a dark suit with blue patterned tie, he grins and tells one journalist: "We are very excited. The performance is good. Growth is good. The debt levels are good. Now I think that the problems belong to everyone else."

Next to him, two of Vodafone's press team whisper conspiratorially. One of them listens intently as his colleague explains how relieved he is with the media reception of the figures. The latter says: "Most of it's gone really well. The BBC: well, they seemed a bit doubtful, but there you go. You can't have everything."

The lobby leading to the ballroom is full of journalists, eyeing the available canapés warily and each other even more so. The analysts have arrived early. They have grabbed the only seats available and are busy poring over the half year data.

Vodafone's PR people are standing en masse at the Ballroom entrance to prevent anyone getting in to seem HIM before the conference is starts. Time and again, journalists approach the door, only to be ushered away by a smartly dressed minder: "We don't think he's quite ready yet. You can't go in to see him just yet. He'll be a few minutes yet. Sorry."

Suddenly the minder's efforts are wasted. The double doors burst open and out from the Ballroom strides Sir Christopher Gent, chief executive of Vodafone. He leans back slightly as he walks, accentuating a slight paunch on an otherwise slim frame. The paunch, you sense, is stretching his black pinstripe trousers, dark blue braces and striped shirt well beyond the comfort zone. A mass of cables is hanging down from his side – clearly Gent is miked up and ready to perform, but heading in the wrong direction.

The lobby suddenly goes quiet, but Gent doesn't pause to look at anyone in the room and strides through in a blur. Where is he going? The men's room, as it turns out. A couple of seasoned journalists, clearly well trained in the art of the mobile interview, instinctively move to pursue him. But on guessing his destination they hastily back-pedal and rejoin the throng. In his absence, the minder realizes the press are probably a safer proposition inside the Ballroom than outside. It's time to head in.

When Gent returns to his seat, journalists are still jostling for position. With a few minutes still to go, the latest advertising campaign is playing on the large screens behind the podium. The slogan "How are You?" is spattered across the walls. Gent, on hearing the ad's music, "Bohemian

Like You" by the Dandy Warhols, starts to click his fingers, tap his feet and smooth back his greying hair. His expression is serious – business is about to be attended to – but he can't suppress a slight smirk when talking to a colleague. In an instant it is gone and the mask returns.

Gent has a cold and cough. Though clearly pumped up for what is about to follow, he takes out his hankie for a quick blow of his nose before the presentation begins. Finally, a press officer tells him that it is time to start. Gent nods his head in assent. The Dandy Warhols are unceremoniously stopped in full flow and Gent pushes himself up, pressing his palms into his thighs, and springs onto the stage. He clears his throat to speak.

Facing his audience, Gent suddenly seems to have moved into a different gear. His MCC tie of blue, red and green diagonal stripes and the silver buckles on his braces gleam under a harsh spotlight. Gent is not a natural public speaker but today he has good news to deliver to his audience. He faces two pencil-thin fixed microphones in front of him. To each side is a glass autocue, a concession to the age when looking good on television is everything. He squeezes the sides of the lectern so tightly that the skin around his hands turns white. But Gent moves doggedly through his pre-sentation, staring grimly into his autocue. Towards the end of his introductions, Gent suddenly stoops behind the lectern and drinks from a glass of water. The cough has returned. He takes a few seconds before con-tinuing. A couple of minutes later, he hands over to his Group Chief Operating Officer, Julian Horn-Smith.

Horn-Smith is a different proposition altogether. He is wearing a smart grey suit with a pale blue shirt and red patterned tie. His face is character-ized by ruddy cheeks, heavy eyelids and thick bushy eyebrows. He speaks clearly but his lips barely seem to move. By contrast to Gent, he seems more relaxed at the podium. No squeezing the lectern for him.

When emphasizing a point, he instead moves both hands up and down simultaneously as if shaking hands with two people at the same time. He takes plenty of opportunities to look out beyond the spotlight and catch the eye of a member of the audience.

Horn-Smith has plenty to say, but Gent isn't really interested in his No. 2's speech. He's heard some, if not all of it, before. Instead, he periodically splutters into his hankie, taps his feet impatiently, wiggles his thighs from side to side and then fiddles with his smart rectangular cufflinks. Just after pulling at the knots on his black lace-up shoes, he looks at a colleague seated at the back of the Ballroom and smirks again.

The Vodafone executives sitting in the front row are not really listening to Horn-Smith either. Thomas Geitner, in his late forties, is playing with his new "Vodafone live!" phone. He seems to be sending photos backwards and forwards to an unknown recipient, and not to be paying the slightest attention. To his left, Peter Bamford, responsible for operations in northern Europe, the Middle East and Africa, keeps opening and shutting his briefcase as if he is about to leave. The furrows in his brow are visible from some distance away. The other executives, all wearing dark suits and all seemingly in their forties or early fifties, seem unable to sit still for long. To a man (and they are only men) they seem vaguely distracted.

Then a momentary farce. When Horn-Smith finishes, the sound engineers at the back of the Ballroom forget to turn Gent's microphone back on. When Ken Hydon, the finance director, congratulates Horn-Smith in a whisper, the two start to giggle and the whole room can hear them. Gent, meanwhile, has begun mouthing his summing up but no one can hear. The problem is rectified within seconds but the image of the slick corporate presentation is briefly lost.

Overall, however, Gent seems in good form. Only when talking about 3G technology does he seem a little hesitant. This is a subject on which he has already been heavily criticized. Perhaps he wonders whether the media will pick on this line today. To help him deal with their questions, he is joined on stage by Horn-Smith and Hydon. The ample Horn-Smith moves behind a desk, fills his swivel chair and looks the part. The smaller Hydon, however, perches on the edge of his seat and dips his toes to find the ground, like a child in an adult's chair.

Then the questions begin. Gent is robust with his inquisitors. He seems magnificently testy, as if wanting to say "What's wrong with you people? What more do you want?" He abruptly reminds one questioner from the *Daily Express* that he has failed to identify himself before asking a question. To another he puts both hands in his back pockets, leans back on the podium and lets out a loud sigh of exasperation. Gent is not slow to throw a barb or two. He tosses one in the direction of "our friends at Vivendi", a reference to an acrimonious battle developing for control of Cegetel. After taking a another sideswipe at Vodafone's competitors, Orange and mmO$_2$, he rolls his tongue across the inside of his cheek and then grins mischievously.

As the press conference draws to a close I ask Gent the final question.

Question: There have been recent rumours about long-term succession planning for your position within Vodafone. But, given these results, do you plan to go on and on and on?

Answer: [laughs] I've always made it clear that that's not the case. I'm a steward of the company rather than a permanent incumbent, BUT [emphasizes word] there's plenty of things to do with this business. It's performing extremely well and I'm having a great time. Given that we're making a lot of progress on impor-

tant initiatives, I don't think that you'll see me out of the door quite as quickly as maybe you hope [suddenly quickens pace of delivery]. Just to say, succession planning is an important issue . . . and I'm sure that the main board will have in mind what it thinks it needs to do on the timescales I've discussed with them about the future. There's plenty to do in this business, it's really going places."

On the face of it, then, it seemed that at 12:58 pm on Tuesday November 12, 2002 Gent was not about to leave. But I wasn't looking at him as he spoke. My tape recorder was taking care of Gent's words, while a look around at his potential internal successors told a far more interesting story. Horn-Smith, sitting behind Gent on the stage, begins to blush furiously. Next to him, Hydon stretches his toes ballerina-style in an effort to touch the ground, perhaps to make sure it's still there. Geitner stops his picture messaging tomfoolery and stiffens his back. Even Bamford ceases fiddling with the contents of his bag. In fact, the whole of the front row of Vodafone executives, once absent-mindedly fooling, fiddling and mumbling through the conference were now noticeable by their rapt attention to their leader's words.

Their reaction was as intriguing as what Gent said. Why his team were suddenly so engrossed is difficult to tell, even today. Were they, depending on their position within the company, either simply disappointed or elated by the face value of his comments? Or did they already know that soon there would be a much bigger story to be told?

At the end of it all, Gent pauses to receive congratulations from colleagues. He strides off the platform knowing that Vodafone has produced unanswerable results. He has every reason to feel pleased with himself and knows that for the first time in a while, the headlines the next day will be good ones.

The six years of Gent's tenure had been a massive rollercoaster ride for both Vodafone and himself. After taking over as Vodafone chief executive in January 1997, he enjoyed huge success in developing it into an international powerhouse through a series of daring global acquisitions. When the technology bubble burst, Gent and Vodafone took a seriously scary and prolonged downward plunge on the rollercoaster. Stocks slid to less than a quarter of the peak value and big questions were raised over his stewardship of his company.

Not any more. Sir Christopher Gent was back. But for how long?

PART 1

On the Up

Here Come the Buccaneers

A trip back in time to Vodafone's birth is a nostalgic tour of all the smells, sights and sounds of rampant Thatcherite entrepreneurialism. Fortune, in all senses of the word, really did favour the brave who tested themselves in a market economy which thrived on deregulation and the sudden emergence of new business opportunities.

Vodafone was one of those brave companies and its leaders saw themselves as buccaneers charting out virgin territory in their field. Two particular buccaneers became knights. In the early days of Vodafone, plain old Ernest Harrison and Gerald Whent believed wholeheartedly in the Thatcherite creed and Vodafone enjoyed a cosy, some would say too cosy, relationship with the successive Conservative governments of Margaret Thatcher and John Major. Harrison and Whent took great care that those that they recruited came in their mould – that they were "one of us", as the British Prime Minister once famously remarked during a battle with those she called the "wets" in her cabinet. Indeed, one of the men that they hired to achieve a revolution in mobile communications was a former leader of the British Young Conservatives, a young, bespectacled grammar-school boy by the name of Christopher Gent.

Although Gent was to go on to transform Vodafone out of all recognition when he took up the reins of the business in 1997, he was only able to do so as a result of those who preceded him in charge of the company. Back in the early 1980s it seemed somewhat far-fetched, even to Harrison and Whent, that in a matter of a few years mobile phones would be in the hands of hundreds of millions of people across the world. Nevertheless both had spent a working lifetime making pots of money for Vodafone's early parent company, Racal.

Ernest Harrison

Ernest Harrison – who became better known as "Ernie" to friends, associates, investors and media alike in the course of his 50 years at Racal – was born in 1926, one year after Margaret Thatcher, in Hackney, London. He was the son of a docker at a time when the capital city was still very much the trading port around which the British Empire conducted much of its business. Ernie's father worked hard and encouraged his son to do the same at school.

In spite of his lowly background, Harrison thrived in an academic environment. A bright student, his teachers found that he was exceptionally strong at maths. Ernie took full advantage of his natural gifts. This, plus an interest in the world of business, meant that he chose to become an accountant. First of all Harrison had to endure a spell of National Service (the two year period of military service that, following the end of the second world war, all young British men were obliged to undertake – the practice ended in the 1960s). On his return from duty, he joined the top accountancy firm George A. Touche, which became Touche Ross and, several mergers later, is today better known to the world as Deloitte & Touche. It was here that young Harrison got the necessary grounding to shape him for a lifetime in business.

Harrison was doing well but wanted to move a little closer to the action end of the business world. It wasn't an easy step for him to convince others that, as an accountant, he had the right character to make an impact on that wider world. He approached, but was rebuffed by, Smiths Industries. Soon, however, another opportunity arose. This time he was approached, by Ray Brown and Calder Cunningham. The pair had formerly worked for Plessey and had recently begun a new venture. Over many hours, they had failed to decide what their new business venture should be called. In the end, in an interesting parallel to the emergence of the name Vodafone many years later, they chose to combine the first letters of their names – and got Racal.

Brown and Cunningham had impeccable engineering backgrounds and admirable business zeal but they knew their limitations. They had little appetite for the nitty-gritty of numbers, so they needed Harrison to complete their team. By 1951, they knew they had found the right man. Harrison became the company secretary and chief accountant.

As Racal's thirteenth employee, it could hardly be said that Harrison was at the centre of a vast empire. Nevertheless, business was growing rapidly. The company's main business was making radio communication units for the military. In an era when the words "ethics" and "business" were rarely used together Racal had few qualms over how it made its money. Not only was it in the military field, but its radio units were based around technology pioneered in the research labs of the apartheid regime in South Africa.

If Harrison was ever bothered during this politically-unconscious time by such deals, he never showed it. His star was in the ascendancy and before the 1950s were out he had joined the 12-strong Racal board. By 1961, when Racal executives had chosen to float the company on the stock market, he had risen to deputy managing director. Then, in 1966, he was appointed chairman of Racal.

Under Harrison the culture of the company changed. Businesses always find their own way of motivating those around them: some motivate by fear and others through camaraderie. Racal, under Harrison, was very much of the latter school.

Furthermore, by the time of Harrison's tenure at Racal, many of its managers had been together for a long time. One of those who worked with Harrison at that time says that Harrison's Racal had an "an invigorating, sort of buccaneering spirit about it". Others talk about hard work and long hours, but also about a really strong sense of team spirit and occasional frenzied bouts of wild corporate partying to celebrate this or that deal being in the bag or targets being met. Part of the team spirit was fostered by Harrison's love of the bizarre. He longed to play practical jokes on his colleagues. On one occasion he colluded with a travelling circus visiting the area to interrupt a cricket match in which his Racal colleagues were playing. At a crucial stage of the match, three elephants duly strayed onto the field of play, leaving players and spectators bewildered.

The company had a close-knit family feel, almost Mafia-like in its intensity. It was no surprise that over the years of hard work and even harder play, that some bright spark coined a new term for Racal executives. They came to be known both inside and outside the company as the "Rafia".

Gerald Whent

A key element of the Harrison Rafia was his long-time colleague Gerry Whent. It was Whent, as chairman of the Racal Radio Group, who brought the business opportunity that was to lead to Vodafone to Harrison's attention. Whent was already well known within Racal as a man who could spot and take advantage of new opportunities and sell them to anyone who had the money to pay for them. He had thrown himself with enthusiasm into selling Racal's military radios to super-wealthy Arab oil sheikhs in the 1970s.

While Harrison's family background was a civilian one, Gerald Arthur Whent's family was deeply ingrained in military service. Whent was born in Ferozepore in 1927, in the Punjab state in the North-West of India. Built around the Sutlej River and near to what would become the Pakistani border, Ferozepore had become a transportation hub and district administrative centre for the British Empire.

The military were there to keep control of vast trading supplies of cotton and grain. Whent's father was a colonel and his brothers all went into the military. He was the fourth child in the family and was sent to a boarding school – St Mary's College, Southampton – from the age of eleven. Whent made little lasting impression on the academic system but showed that he had plenty of the necessary qualities for a career in business. "I was not very bright, but I was always the leader of the gang," he would recall later.

Like Harrison, Whent had to take the medicine of National Service. Once he had emerged, he got a steady job. His early career was far removed from selling electronic kit. He was attracted by the prospect of becoming a management trainee with Dent Allcroft, a glove maker.

By 1962, he knew everything there was to know about making the perfect glove for customers. Now in his mid-thirties and not having achieved a great deal, a frustrated Whent enviously eyed the dynamic growth industry of electronics. He blagged his way into a job at Plessey, the same company from which Racal's founders Brown and Cunningham had emerged. His move into Racal came without the need for a job interview. He went from Plessey to Controls & Communications. And when Controls & Communications was taken over by Racal, Whent found himself at the centre of something altogether more exciting than making gloves.

Harrison quickly saw Whent's eye for an opportunity and moved him into radio communications, Racal's most dynamic growth area. His successes in the area impressed the Racal board and eventually led to a promotion to the chairmanship of the Racal Radio Group, a major division of Racal Electronics. Once in a position of power, Whent continually harangued an initially sceptical board into looking at mobile phone communications, something which eventually led to the creation of Vodafone.

Whent epitomized the Rafia management style fostered by Harrison. By nature he was a buccaneer in Harrison's mould and wasn't in the slightest bit aloof. Whent described himself as a "benign dictator" and most of those who worked with him could only agree.

The benign part of his character was easy enough to spot. Whent positively dripped with enthusiasm every day he turned up for work. He was loved for his encouragement of those around him. Perhaps because of his concern for his staff, allied to a good sense of humour, Whent was a hugely popular figure at Racal and was able to command great loyalty from those around him. Gent recalls: "Gerry was a hugely popular chief executive and . . . he had a tremendous sense of humour and a great enthusiasm for the business, its people and life." Had the phrase "larger than life" not already existed, it would have had to have been invented for him.

Whent was committed to corporate entertaining. Many years later Chris Gent would recall this: "He was a great believer in entertaining and his generous hospitality on racecourses and golf courses throughout the UK led to long-standing friendships with suppliers, customers and colleagues." When it came to sponsorship of sport, Whent had a more-than-willing boss to sign the cheques. Harrison's passion for football was well known. His North London background had made him a lifelong Arsenal season ticket holder and investor, and he shared Whent's passion for horse racing, which eventually resulted in Vodafone's sponsorship of the Derby.

Certainly, Whent believed in good living rather than bottled water lunches, declaring that while his military father had had "champagne tastes and beer money", he himself had "champagne money and beer taste". This was only partly true, as he delighted in smoking fat cigars and driving a Rolls-Royce. Whent's all-consuming interest in work and play came at a heavy price: his marriage to Coris Bellman-Thomas produced one son and one daughter but was dissolved. By 1985 he had inherited another three stepchildren through his second wife Sarah, whom he married in that year.

While Whent relished the good life, perhaps a little too much, the dictatorial part of his character was never that far away. He had an undoubted authoritarian streak and his drive was clear for everyone to see as he pushed his division of Racal forward relentlessly, determined to see his ideas put into practice. Whent was completely intolerant of anybody foolish enough to get in the way of those ideas. Even Gent, his young protégé in the early days of Vodafone, admitted that "on occasions he could be slightly dogmatic".

He was undoubtedly in control of his part of the Racal business and always wanted to be seen to be involved, in the thick of the action. When it was suggested to him, years after Vodafone had set up its Newbury headquarters, that he would be better off moving his office back to Racal's head office in Bracknell, Whent was horrified. He refused point blank, saying he would never move away from the business hub.

Whent's "work hard, play hard" character was still to the fore well into his mid-fifties. One has to admire the fact that when most people of his age would have been thinking about winding down for retirement, Whent was ready and waiting for what was to become the busiest period of his life. When Whent's big chance arrived, however, it came more by the way of good fortune than anything else.

The start of it all

In the late summer of 1982, with a deadline for applications for a second cellular telephone network less than the month away (the first was held by Cellnet, a consortium of British Telecom and Securicor), an electronics entrepreneur visited Whent, who was running Racal's military radio business, to discuss its potential.

Whent was receptive but non-committal: he listened to what the expert had to say, but his mind was on other things. He had to make a important trip to Racal's Australian business the following week. Whent recalled that at the time he was extremely busy, but liked enough of what he heard to ask others to check the facts around cellular in his absence: "I saw [the expert] and then briefed my staff to look at the technology and the market here while I went off for a week to visit our Australian company."

Although Whent didn't himself reveal the identity of his visitor, Vodafone sources confirm that it was the late Jan Stenbeck, one of whose interests was the Millicom Group. Following Stenbeck's recent death his obituary claimed that it was he who had given Whent the idea of the mobile phone. After inheriting his father's forestry and engineering business, Stenbeck took an opportunistic tip to the UK, arriving unannounced in Whent's office. He told him about a new "cellular" phone technology that relied on short wave communications to a transmitter which would communicate automatically from "cell to cell". Whent had never heard of the technology but headed off to Australia keen to return as soon as possible.

In his absence, Whent's team had been hard at work researching their new area of interest; on his return, Whent became convinced that cellular was a business that they should be in. Even the formidable Whent was a little hesitant: it was a massive challenge, not least because Racal had no knowledge of either telecoms or the mass-marketing techniques necessary to sell a cellular telephone. But the potential revenues estimated by his team, which later proved to be a fraction of cellular's real earnings, removed any lingering doubts.

Whent visited Harrison – in London. One of Harrison's idiosyncrasies was that because Racal did not have a London office, he kept a permanent suite at the Dorchester where he enjoyed "receiving" business visitors and being generally treated like royalty. As they sat down and discussed the matter in one of his rooms, Harrison quickly became convinced that the idea had merit. A few days later, Whent was sufficiently persuasive to convince the Racal Electronics Group Board that it should bid for the licence.

Once approval for a bid had been granted, Racal put together its proposal for a cellular network. Whent was pleased with the proposal, which was submitted with a few days to spare. As any businessman or investment banker will tell you, however, it is rare for submissions to go without some last minute hitch, which generates panic in its wake. Whent's moment of panic came with only a day to go before the bid's first deadline. He was told that if he persisted in bidding with a 40% stake from a foreign equity partner (in this case the Millicom Group) then Racal stood no chance at all of making a successful bid. In a frenzied couple of hours spent haggling with its partners, Whent negotiated them down to 15% (and later acquired them), with Racal at 80% and Hambros taking up the remaining 5%. Ultimately, it made little difference to the Americans, who still made a lot of money. Many years later Stenbeck reportedly cashed in his stake in Vodafone for £120m.

Once this obstacle had been overcome, Racal found itself one of three groups to be shortlisted for a second round of bids. But with no experience in the telecoms business, Racal was still at this stage seen very much as a rank outsider in the bidding process. The second round went on for a whole week, with Whent and his team locked into a suite of hotel rooms at the Sheraton Hotel Heathrow with a small army of American Millicom officials, technical advisors and bankers from Hambros, and a team from Saatchi & Saatchi. But it was the promise from the bidding team to spend heavily on building a cellular network that really impressed their government inquisitors. Whent was prepared to spend large amounts on building the networks because his forecasts were considerably more bullish than those of any of his rival bidders. Ultimately, Racal's friends in the Conservative government wanted to believe that its cellular licences would be a success and so Racal got the go ahead.

Whent was only able to make such promises because Harrison was prepared to authorize such spending without any quibbles. This was particularly impressive, as Harrison at the time was being severely criticized in the City for Racal's sluggish growth rate. Harrison was prepared to face further criticism by bankrolling Whent on a new and unproven venture, because he knew that you don't make money without taking chances. And he knew his man. From working together and playing together as part of the Rafia, Harrison knew he could trust Whent's gut instinct. With the licence safely in their pocket, Harrison and Whent knew that they were on the start of a rollercoaster ride. What they couldn't have known was just how phenomenal the ride would be.

The birth of Vodafone

Whent immediately set up the new company, known until 1986 as Racal Millicom, to develop and implement the analogue network. Headquarters were based in the pleasant market town of Newbury, Berkshire, with 50 employees in one building. The venture needed a new name. After several days of thought, one seemed to Whent to fit much better than any other. While bidding for and winning the right to use the licence, Whent had argued that the use of mobiles would extend to data as well as voice services. The combination of VO-ice and DA-ta mobile communication gave the name Vodafone.

Even though Racal had never been in this line of business before, Harrison realized that his cooperation didn't start and end with a successful bid. He, like Whent, saw the potential of the idea and knew that it was important to commit the right level of resources to the project. Many years later he revealed: "We knew cellular was going to be a big business, so we bid for the licence, we won it and we put everything into it – all our money, all our best people. We made that a success by intensity of purpose. There is no doubt in life that intensification in a niche area, with everything going into that, is how you are going to win."

The management at Vodafone reflected this intensity, which was just as well because there were a lot of problems in developing the network. Many early problems centred on the helter-skelter pace of growth. There were difficulties with planning permission for building the base stations necessary for the cellular network and this in turn threatened delays and call congestion. In spite of furious lobbying by its rival Cellnet, Vodafone was temporarily given more radio channels to solve the problem. In the course of the two years after winning the licence, Whent poured £800m into the building the physical network necessary to make the service work.

Enter Chris Gent

Before long, Whent realized that he needed fresh blood in Vodafone to maintain the project's impetus. The location at Newbury was crucial: Whent knew that here he could attract the high-calibre management talent that he needed to make the fledgling Vodafone work. He went to Plessey for many telecoms experts and headhunted those with the necessary marketing know-how from other computer and electronics companies. Above all, however, the team Whent needed to make all of this happen would be energetic and in the prime of their business lives; people in their late thirties or early forties. One such person on the short list of Whent's headhunter was a young man by the name of Christopher Gent.

Whent had received the CVs of many hopefuls for a senior management position at the new company. Some seemed promising to him, others deeply disappointing, and CVs passed across his desk for several months. Most of the time they stayed in a pile on his desk while he chased his tail in the months of frenzied activity once Vodafone had won its licence. At last, after yet another phone call from the headhunter reminding him of the latest batch of hopefuls, Whent settled down to sort wheat from chaff. He later recalled the moment his eyes first fixed on the name "Christopher Gent". He read the CV carefully and quickly put it in the wheat pile before moving on. A few weeks later, after seeing Gent for himself, he knew that he had unearthed a "good 'un". "I can remember being impressed straight away," said Whent. "I worked harder on getting him than I did on most people. Of course, though, it helped that we were able to offer him a more senior position and more money."

More seniority and more money was something that Gent had been becoming used to over the previous few years. His dramatic rise to prominence was all the more remarkable given his humble origins. Christopher Gent was born on a naval estate in Gosport, Hampshire, on May 10, 1948. His father was a chief petty officer while his mother had to get used to living in a household full of men: there were Gent's three brothers as well as his father. The family grew up in Dulwich, an area of South London. Two of Gent's brothers were sent to public school but young Christopher was packed off to the local grammar school. Every day, Gent took a long trip on a No. 3 bus across south London to the all-boys Archbishop Tenison School, near the Oval cricket ground.

Gent's daily trip may have been inconvenient, but once he got there he was situated in the best possible place for his fledgling interest in cricket. His love for the game had much to do with the location of the school. One teacher at Tenison recounts that in Gent's time the braver pupils used to climb on the school roof to watch matches at lunchtime. This practice was brought to an abrupt end when one pupil (not Gent but, according to one report, Tony Banks, who went on to become the sports minister in Tony Blair's Labour government) loudly heckled Dennis Compton during a quiet period in a key match.

The arrival of cricketers in their whites each spring was a welcome sign for the young Gent. Cricket meant better weather and the eventual arrival of the summer school holidays. For apart from listening to the sound of leather on willow, Gent thoroughly detested being at school. He was utterly miserable and failed to shine in any way, shape or form. "I wasn't very academic," he admitted many years later. "I found school so demotivating and uninteresting that I didn't develop any particular interests."

It wasn't just that Gent hated school. Many at the school seemed to hate him. Already lacking confidence through his unspectacular classroom achievements, things got far worse when several Tenison pupils were suspected of having vandalized one of the many local trains chuntering into and out of the main London stations each day. When the perpetrators were caught, it was suspected that the young Gent, having received information on who was to blame, had told those in authority.

Gent maintained that he had not "told" on anybody, but it made no difference. He was routinely beaten up, bullied and shunned by his classmates for 18 months. Many years later, Gent explained that he was happier to suffer in silence than try and persuade others of his innocence. The experience definitely affected him for some time after. "The whole thing wasn't particularly good at the time," he recalled. "It's quite difficult to have a satisfactory school career when you're not talking to anybody."

The No. 3 bus trip back from Tenison's to Dulwich was a far happier experience. At its end, he could retreat into the warmth of his family home, a much happier environment than the traumas of school. It was here Gent's natural, rather than academic, intelligence developed. In particular this was a family that loved to talk about anything, from what they had been doing that day to the weighty issues in the news. His father, though battling against poor health, held lively political debates around the family dinner table and young Gent was expected to give as good as he got.

The bullying eventually eased off and Gent started to show sufficient signs of alertness in the classroom for him to consider whether he should go to university.

But then his father died after a lengthy battle against cancer. Although not a huge surprise, it left the whole family utterly distraught. Gent decided to forsake the chance of university, which could have left him miles from his family at a difficult time.

Instead, he headed straight into the workforce. In 1967, at the age of nineteen, he took a job as a trainee at Britain's National Westminster Bank. It was around this time in his life that Chris Gent became friendly with a young man by the name of John Major. The future chief executive of Vodafone got on like a house on fire with the future British Prime Minister. They had extraordinarily similar backgrounds. Gent, an unhappy schoolboy in the Oval; Major, whose youthful ambitions were thwarted by his family's grinding poverty in Brixton; Gent, who watched Surrey's finest play from his school vantage point; Major, who had to save pocket money in the winter months to watch his heroes at the Oval in the summer. Gent, whose father's life had ebbed away when his son was in his late teens; Major, who had lost his father at around the same age; Gent, who was attracted to National Westminster by the prospect of a steady job and a respectable career; Major, who was drawn to Standard Chartered for exactly the same reasons.

Yet the thing that really drew them together was a shared interest in politics. Both were keen young Conservatives in the late 1960s, at a time when conservatism was the last thing on the minds of most young men and women. Major and Gent were definitely not stereotypical swinging-sixties types, seeming to be more concerned with the free market than free love. But, as Major described in his highly readable autobiography, "The Brixton Young Conservatives were then a merry and growing band . . . we canvassed, enrolled new members, helped in political campaigns, held dances and tennis mornings, went on outings, published our own magazine, heckled local Labour MPs and thoroughly enjoyed ourselves."

Gent and Major found a bond and remain friends to this day. The two have been known to travel together to see the British cricket team play. The friendship also demonstrated a knack that Gent seemed to have of meeting the right people at the right time. Robert Atkins, a close friend of Gent's and a former Conservative sports minister, says: "The fact that Chris got to know John Major when he was young could be seen as good luck, but in reality he was always ahead of the game. He was an out-and-out networker, in the positive sense of the word. He got to know the kind of people who would give him the right kind of information. He never does anything that isn't calculated."

Both Gent and Major were passionate about their politics. Major got invaluable experience as a councillor in Brixton but it was Gent who seemed at the time to have the much greater potential for a career in politics. Admired by his peers, he rose swiftly up the ranks of the Young Conservatives and by the late 1970s had become its Chairman.

Gent did all the things that a gifted young politician should do. He served as a member of the Conservative Party's National Union Executive Committee as well as being on several other Committees. He worked as an assistant to a leading Conservative politician; he certainly flirted with the idea of running for Parliament and becoming an MP.

But something was holding him back. He loved his politics and some speculate that he would have been talented enough to have risen to ministerial level in the new right wing Conservative party reinvigorated by the election of Margaret Thatcher as its leader in 1975. Others are less sure, claiming that Gent would never have cut the mustard because he was an unfashionably "wet" conservative at a time when the Tories were becoming drier than a desert.

No one will ever know, but perhaps for Gent politics wasn't the be all and end all. Unlike Major, he had an alternative path to follow; he had been assiduously climbing the corporate as well as the political ladder. In 1979 he joined Baric, a computer services company jointly owned by Barclays and ICL. Initially, he was a market development manager, but rose rapidly to managing director level. He shared some of his time there with Peter (later Sir Peter) Bonfield, who was later to become chief executive of British Telecommunications. As chief executive of Vodafone, he would later to show Sir Peter a thing or two about global expansion. Gent also later worked with Sir Robin Biggam, who chaired BICC and is now the Independent Television Commission chairman.

Even though he chose to follow the path of business rather than politics, it is clear that Gent had built good political contacts. This was something that would undoubtedly have been noticed by the Thatcherite Whent, himself a significant donor to the Conservative Party at Vodafone, as he surveyed Gent's CV. The two men met and it was clear that each had something to offer the other. For Whent, Gent was a clearly capable younger man who he could rely on to drive the Vodafone agenda onwards. For Gent, Whent was a wily entrepreneurial buccaneer from whom he could learn much in an exciting and rapidly growing market. And he got to come in on more money as Vodafone's managing director.

There is little doubt that Gent's political contacts within the Thatcher and Major Conservative governments came in handy when Vodafone needed to lobby its cause. Not that this was a company or industry facing the problems of decline as seen in the coal, steel or manufacturing industries in the 1980s. Far from it: telecoms was at the start of what was to prove a long boom period.

On January 1, 1985 Vodafone hosted the first ever mobile call in the UK, made from St Katherine's Dock in London to Vodafone's base in

Newbury. The call was initiated by the comedian Ernie Wise of More-cambe & Wise. Although in retrospect, with countless millions of mobile phones now sold around the world, his words could have been as almost as significant as those spoken by Neil Armstrong on landing on the moon, it seems that nobody can quite remember exactly what he said at what was effectively a publicity stunt on a cold day when most of the UK was sleeping off the effects of celebrating New Year. Hopefully it wasn't along the lines of "I'm at the docks" or "Sorry, you'll have to speak up" but was something a little more profound . . .

Although few noticed the event at the time, this was the first cellular net-work to launch in the UK. After the launch, the network was rolled out rapidly. Whent and his Vodafone team were taking the massive gamble of investing heavily in building the network's range, but after the launch it soon became obvious to all that Vodafone had launched the right service to the right market at exactly the right time. This was the start of good times for the UK's young urban professionals ("yuppies"). Fuelled by a Thatcherite belief in the power of market forces, many young men and women were making good money in business. They saw even the cumbersome mobile handsets in production at that time as an essential new status symbol, one every bit as essential as the best champagne or a fast car.

The terms of the cellular licence prevented Vodafone from selling its ser-vice direct to the public. So Vodac, the Group's wholly owned subsidiary, was formed to be a service provider for the fledgling network. The lack of a consumer outlet didn't particularly bother Whent, who had made a decision some time earlier to go for the big business markets first, busi-nesses who would provide their staff with a means of contact with the office whether they were out at meetings or at play. The early growth of the network reflected the likely location of the high-fliers. London and all the major cities in the UK were connected up very quickly, as well as certain obvious playgrounds of the rich such as polo pitches and the yacht harbours of the Solent.

Under Whent, Vodafone proved itself more agile, inventive and ruthless than its lumbering competition at Cellnet. Although Vodafone's initial target was to gain 30% market share it found itself up above 50% within a few years. At this point Vodafone had become the world's largest cellular network. It had over 165,000 network subscribers already signed up using their car or hand phones, and another 2,000 joining each week. By May 1998, the network was handling more than 7 million calls in a week and had achieved a 90% coverage of the country a full two years ahead of its 1990 target, with only remote areas such as the Scottish Highlands left uncovered.

The growth of the company continued to outperform even the most optimistic projections of the original business plan. At this stage there were a couple of important developments that helped its growth further. Vodata was created to develop and market Vodafone Recall, the voicemail service, and other value-added services were gradually included, such as the first information lines from the likes of the Financial Times CityLine and AA Roadwatch. Vodapage was also launched, which provided a paging network that covered 80% of the UK population. All these developments served to reinforce the growth of the Vodafone network as something that was becoming genuinely indispensable rather than just a gimmick for the rich.

Back at Racal, the success of Vodafone was starting to dominate Ernie Harrison's boardroom agenda. The Racal Telecom Division had moved from a far-flung part of his empire to centre stage and was by now accounting for about a third of Racal's annual profits. Harrison, as a numbers man, knew a good opportunity to make some quick money when he saw it. And this was as obvious an opportunity as any he had seen. Racal was keen to make a profit from the growing mobile sector and floated 20% of the ordinary share capital of the Telecom division on both the London and the New York stock exchanges.

The performance of Vodafone and its partial flotation was quickly reflected in the wage packets of the directors. In August 1989, at the company's first annual meeting, Whent and his colleagues awarded themselves pay rises of up to 155%, plus share option schemes, while paying a final dividend of only 0.7p. The decision unleashed shareholder fury over the pay packets of Harrison and Whent similar to that which was to tarnish Chris Gent's reputation in the media many years later. One disgruntled shareholder said: "It's scandalous. I know the directors have done a good job, but what about us? It indicates a certain amount of avarice." Unfortunately for this and other shareholders, this was not only an era when shareholders were less well organized in voicing their dissent, but was also one when avarice was held to be a virtue rather than a deadly sin.

Even so the uproar was sufficient for the directors to feel the need to defend themselves in public. Whent was a particular target for criticism, as he had received the largest increase. Harrison (who had bumped up his own pay by 24%) jumped to his defence, reminding shareholders that the salary of directors was not high by international standards. "These executives have earned every penny of their remuneration," he said. "They have turned in a fantastic performance in the past six years, boosting the value of the company to £3.5 billion. We need to retain profit to have the working capital we need to develop into a great worldwide telecommunications leader. Shareholders are looking for capital gains, not the dissipation of profits through higher dividends."

Demerger

Whether or not that really was what shareholders were looking for, most kept their grumblings to themselves. Whent and Harrison were becoming favourites in the City and the promise of overseas expansion meant lots of jam tomorrow. This jam came in the form of a flotation. By 1991 Vodafone had emerged as an independent company, listed on the London and New York Exchanges. Racal and Vodafone decided to demerge fully in what at the time was the largest demerger in UK corporate history. The potential for Vodafone was there for all to see. The company's digital (GSM) mobile phone service was launched – the first in the UK. The company had won its independence, and Whent repaid Harrison's faith with soaring sales and profits. Harrison was still chairman, but Whent, at 64 years of age, was now the chief executive of a major public company. He pushed it on and on in his own special Vodafone version of the "Rafia" work hard, play hard approach which endeared him to the by now rapidly growing number of employees working for him.

When the flotation came, everyone in senior management at Vodafone became rich beyond their wildest dreams. Whent paused to reflect on his success in driving the business forward combined with his undoubted good fortune of being in the right market at the right time. "There's never been a business like it," he said. "From nothing to £3.5 billion in seven years has got to be manna from Heaven."

Manna from heaven maybe, but it would have gone elsewhere had it not been for Whent. Throughout the period of Vodafone's growth, his special talent was to be able to react quickly to – and even foresee – market developments. He was quicker than anyone to realize that the huge amounts of cash being generated by the company should be used to finance overseas investments. Having founded Vodafone in the UK, he was the quickest to realize that there was no reason why mobile phones shouldn't have similar potential abroad. He began the strategy of expansion with a small partnership in Malta. International partnerships were formed with consortia in Germany, South Africa, Australia, Fiji and Greece. These developments continued with other consortia in the Netherlands, Hong Kong, Germany and France. The company formed Vodafone Group International to acquire licences and supervise overseas interests. And by the time Whent retired in 1996 he had built a presence in 10 countries, although Vodafone had control in only three.

By now, of course, Vodafone had already moved heavily into the mass consumer market from its original, much smaller, business customer base. By 1993, Vodafone had opened its first High Street Vodafone Centre (although its own retail store chain was not to emerge until 1997), and announced its first distribution agreement with the major UK high street retailer Comet. Within two years, over 500 specialist retail outlets and seven high street chains were connecting mobile phones to the Vodafone network. As well as Comet, these were the John Lewis Partnership, AA stores, The Link, Pinnacle Vodafone shops, Talkland and Pocket Phone stores.

By the mid-1990s, Whent knew that the time was approaching for him to go. He was receiving official recognition for his efforts. He was knighted in 1995 and finally retired at the end of the following year. By the time he stepped down, Whent undoubtedly had much to be proud of.

But who would succeed him? By the time Whent moved over, Gent had become the clear front runner, but it hadn't always been obvious that he would get the top job. Between 1985 and 1997, when he took over as chief executive, he had toiled away as managing director and seen major rivals come and go. Those inside Vodafone at that time say he used his former political experience to great effect and was able to elbow rivals aside at important moments. He became known as the "cornjumper" for his ability to step on the toes of his rivals to get to the top. Once there, according to those former rivals, he froze out anyone who was not loyal to him. Whent didn't see Gent as being so ruthless. "Nobody was being groomed to take over as chief executive exactly, but he emerged over time as the most likely successor," he said.

The long, gruelling hours Gent spent getting himself to the top cost him dear in his personal life. His first marriage to Lynda, with whom he had two daughters, broke down and he is now married to his second wife, Kate, with whom he has a young family. After his divorce, Gent saw less of his two teenage daughters. Whent, whose own fanatical dedication to the cause of his career had left him with a broken marriage too, was sympathetic to his successor, saying: "On the surface, he didn't seem too affected by it. But I'm sure that, underneath, it disturbed him a lot."

Almost as soon as Gent became CEO, Whent and Harrison both moved out of the Vodafone spotlight. Whent soon retired but didn't go away altogether. Before his death in 2000, he threw himself into voluntary work in his adopted Newbury. One other project that gave Whent particular pleasure was the creation of a business park on the former site of the Greenham Common airbase – famous for its anti-war women's camp during the 1980s – as a director of the Greenham Common Trust. To Whent this had two enthralling aspects. The first was his bread and butter: the creation of jobs and business. The second was altogether more pleasurable: the eradication of what he saw as a pacifist feminist legacy.

Harrison spent a few more years winding down. Outside work, he was every inch the happy family man. Devoted to his nearest and dearest, he spent most weekends either at the races or with his wife Janie, thinking what to do with a rather rambling garden; there were also five children and a growing number of grandchildren. But he also had Racal to attend to.

He still had an impressively direct way of doing business. Immediately prior to the eventual sale of Racal to Thomson-CSF in early 2000, Harrison was becoming impatient while waiting for Denis Ranque, Thomson-CSF's chairman, to arrive at a meeting. When he turned up, Ranque immediately informed Harrison that he would have to leave soon for another meeting. "Never mind," said Harrison, "I think you left three questions for me from our last meeting. The answers are: yes, no and no. Is that okay?" This brief encounter did Ranque no harm, marking a brief hiccup en route to the purchase of Racal for £2bn. The sale, as Racal marked its fiftieth and final birthday, also marked Harrison's decision to retire – at 73. Brian Newman, who watched the growth of Racal and Vodafone, told the *Sunday Times* on Harrison's retirement in January 2000: "He is the last of the post-war electronics entrepreneurs. If he was starting out today he would have been an internet king." Harrison fostered a reputation as a great negotiator. As one former colleague says: "At poker-dice and spoof, Ernie is lethal. He is also an extraordinary businessman."

Harrison, as he neared retirement following the sale of Racal, had been very concerned to get the right deal not just for him but for everyone connected with what he still called the "Rafia". Harrison said, when he finally sold Racal itself to Thomson-CSF: "As a result of this merger, Racal people will have a big opportunity for the future. I have always felt in business, you have two responsibilities: to the shareholders and to colleagues and employees. You've got to make sure both of these parties benefit from the success."

Also not generally known is the role that Sir Ernest Harrison played in bringing the National Lottery to the UK. It was never publicized at the time, but he had led some important early negotiations with Guy Snowden, the big, bruising, American planning to assemble a powerful UK consortium (he later famously became embroiled with Richard Branson over the former's alleged methods of doing business). Snowden and Harrison both shared a passion for horse racing and regularly went to Sandown Park together, and the result of these earlier deliberations was Camelot. It was Harrison who picked out Tim Holley as a likely chief executive of Camelot, having been impressed by his track record running Racal's data communications division.

But with Harrison and Whent, the buccaneers who founded Vodafone, now gone, Gent was left to run the show. It wasn't long before Gent pushed Vodafone to new heights.

Shy Sam and
Curious Klaus

When Chris Gent took over at Vodafone he was looking to move the group into a different league. Harrison and Whent had built the company out of Racal into a stronger UK performer with at least a foothold in 10 countries. Gent's ambition was to transform the company out of all recognition into a global powerhouse.

First, however, he had a little domestic tidying up to get through. On his promotion to chief executive, Gent looked at his inherited empire and saw a company that had already grown so rapidly that it had not time to think about its structure. So he set about a radical reorganization of Vodafone. Six wholly-owned providers of the Vodafone service were reduced to three – Vodafone Corporate, Vodafone Retail and Vodafone Connect. As a result, the numbers of billing and customer care systems were rationalized, with brands and tariffs streamlined. Vodafone's "Pay as You Talk" digital package was launched, offering no bills, no credit check and no fixed term contract. The launch was a spectacular success. Two years on, the Pay as You Talk package had won over two million customers.

The restructuring of Vodafone was actually a potentially unsettling exercise for the company but those who know Gent well remarked on how well he adapted to his new role in those early months. Having already been at Vodafone for twelve years, he was hardly an unknown quantity, but his style of leadership could not have been more different to that of the garrulous Gerry Whent. Gent's style of leadership was quietly deter-mined. He found his own way of motivating people. Nancy Cobb, Gent's assistant until she retired in September 2002, says: "He is softly spoken, his tone rarely changes and I don't think I have ever seen him flustered. He has a calming influence on the people around him, all of whom are very loyal. He is as considerate about the person who cleans the office as he is to a colleague on the main board. I had always found him to be one of the most charming people one could hope to meet, quiet, always getting on with his job in a forthright way."

Indeed, Gent was so forthright in his commitment to his job that he took to getting up at 5.30 a.m. each morning. This got him into work at 6.30 a.m., with a glass of grapefruit juice waiting as his breakfast. Meetings with senior directors – many of whom had only just crawled out of bed – started at around 7.30 a.m. In the early months of his reign Gent threw himself into his job, spending a lot of time thinking about what he wanted to do. This strategic aspect to his character hugely impresses many who know him well. Sir David Scholey, the former SG Warburg Chairman who is now a Vodafone non-executive director, describes him as a unique com-bination of details man and sweeping visionary: "He keeps the facts at his fingertips but is very clear and decisive." Another banker who has worked closely with Gent says: "I think he is somebody who is very easy to under-estimate. He has a cracking brain and is a thinker as well as a doer."

Gent, however, would have been well advised to have thought a little more about one action six months into his time as CEO. While Gent was now at the top of his particular tree, his old friend John Major was about to fall out of his. The 1997 general election loomed and the Conservative Party seemed to be heading for almost certain defeat at the hands of Tony Blair's New Labour.

For his twelve years at Vodafone and for six years before he arrived, the Conservatives had been in power. Gent and his predecessors had enjoyed long and beneficial associations with the ruling party. The prospect that this association would now end should, to most hard-headed business-men, simply have meant channelling their energies into lobbying a government of new colours.

Although electoral defeat for the Conservatives was a near certainty as the polling day – May 1, 1997 – approached, Gent couldn't resist striking one final blow on behalf of Major and his government. He unwisely rallied 38 business chiefs to put their names to a letter in the *Daily Mail* on the eve of the general election, in which they urged the newspaper's readers to vote Conservative. Gent told the newspaper: "The impression given by Labour is that as far as business is concerned, it does not matter which party wins the election. It is a dangerous myth and that is why we chose to show that we are unequivocal in our support of the Conservatives as the party of business."

The letter seemed a rather futile exercise: readers of the *Daily Mail* were unlikely to do anything other than vote Conservative and the letter did nothing except annoy the incoming government, who swept to power with a thumping majority. Although Gent was impressing many with his handling of Vodafone's internal affairs in the first year of his stewardship of the company, his political touch seemed far less sure.

The episode served to show others and maybe even himself that he had been wise to stay in business rather than venture into politics. It was a mistake that may not have happened had he sought the counsel of Lord MacLaurin. Ian MacLaurin owed his peerage to the recommendation of John Major, but knew that you always had to find ways to deal with the people who would be in power tomorrow rather than today. MacLaurin, at the time of the election a Vodafone board member, was the former chairman of Tesco. He was and still is a formidable businessman who had modernized the retailing giant and emerged victorious from unpleasant scraps with Shirley Porter, the daughter of Lord Cohen, Tesco's founder. Ultimately, as Vodafone chairman from mid-1998, he would become a major civilizing influence on Vodafone's corporate behaviour.

To be fair the letter put Gent out of favour for only a short while, not least because of his unusually pro-European views for a Conservative Party member. Gent has also been scrupulously careful about his political statements since and was noticeably reluctant to get involved in the run up to the 2002 election, when the Conservatives were heavily defeated once more.

External affairs . . . AirTouch

Away from his political misadventures, Gent continued to restructure Vodafone internally. His eye was on opportunities for international expansion. The group had dallied in some ventures in Europe, but lacked a strong presence there. It had interests in Asia but could do better and it had nothing to speak of in North America. While he tidied up what he already had, Gent's mind was already elsewhere: he was looking out for the big one.

When the big one came, however, Gent was as far from the centre of corporate activity as it was possible for anyone to be. His hobby was entirely predictable: he was watching some cricket. His location was somewhat less predictable, though he had been known to travel long distances to attend matches: he was in Australia watching England play their old enemy in the Ashes.

When Gent heard the news at the start of January 1999 that Bell Atlantic and AirTouch, two American telecoms giants, had reached an advanced stage of merger negotiations, he knew that he had to interrupt his holiday. But he only did so to the extent of picking up his mobile in the middle of the test match in Sydney and instructing Ken Hydon, his finance director, to head to New York for face-to-face talks with AirTouch executives – and up the ante. Why? Because Gent too had designs on AirTouch. With Bell Atlantic apparently nearing the finish line, he had to move quickly.

He did, but only to Auckland, the next leg on his holiday. In Newbury and New York, however, other Vodafone executives were sweating it out on his behalf. It was by no means clear, even to his most loyal senior staff at Vodafone, that a Vodafone bid for AirTouch was either logistically possible or even a very good idea. There were obvious reasons to doubt whether Vodafone should be getting involved at all in the mobile business in the United States.

Here was a country which for all its pioneering internet technology, hadn't yet really taken to mobile phones. Mobile licences were not the preserve of a few lucky operators as they were in Europe. There were thousands upon thousands of licences, owned by telecoms giants and the man in the corner store alike. This market was not so much fragmented as splintered into tens of thousands of pieces. Another impediment was that America was still charging mobile phone users for incoming as well as outgoing calls. This meant that penetration rates in the US by the start of 1999 ran at about 1 in 4 of the population. The penetration rate in the UK was about the same but rising much more quickly, while in Finland, the home of Nokia, nearly 60% of the population had mobile phones by this time.

It didn't seem a promising market to be in, yet Gent saw things differently. AirTouch, along with rivals Sprint and McCaw, had begun what he saw as a potential transformation of the American market. They had put in place national tariffs and better network reliability; as a result these operators now seemed to be getting favourable returns on their investments. To Gent, AirTouch's domestic business was a perfect cash-generating business to be involved in. It seemed likely to take out its fragmented smaller rivals sooner rather than later in the domestic market. Gent wasn't about to turn away gifts like that if he could help it.

On the face of it, Vodafone didn't stand a chance with any bid against Bell Atlantic for AirTouch. After all, Gent had been interested in and rebuffed by AirTouch once before. The man who spurned Gent's advance was a shy southerner by the name of Sam Ginn. It was Ginn who, in 1994, had persuaded the board of Pacific Telesis, the phone company of which he was the boss, to spin off a mobile phone part of the business. AirTouch was born, and so confident was Ginn of its potential that he chose to take the helm.

In 1994, the American mobile phone market was even more fragmented than it would be five years later when Gent surveyed the scene. AirTouch was already the largest player and it had barely a tenth of the market. Everything seemed to be up for grabs and Ginn and his team worked ferociously hard to build up a presence in the mobile phone market. The hard work paid off and the business grew rapidly. Before long Ginn looked around for opportunities to replicate the domestic success of AirTouch and started to wonder whether the company could make money abroad. He put together a network of mobile phone licences and joint ventures across Europe and soon had arguably the highest quality network for mobile phones on the continent.

Chris Gent could hardly ignore AirTouch's success in Europe and it was this that originally fuelled his interest in the company. AirTouch's reputation with analysts was nowhere near that of Vodafone but it was still highly respectable. And whenever Gent looked to expand organically or acquire the operations of others in Europe he kept bumping into AirTouch executives who were looking to do precisely the same thing.

AirTouch didn't remotely have Vodafone's clout in Europe, yet as two separate companies they were fighting over similar territory. As a merged company they would have a great fit of existing businesses worldwide and a reasonable chance of boosting revenue and profitability. Better still, AirTouch was big in the United States, an area where Vodafone had little representation. Vodafone and AirTouch personnel were already highly familiar with one another. They were business partners in Egypt and Sweden and co-operated on Globalstar, a satellite-based mobile-phone system. A merger with Vodafone would create a global cellular giant worth around £60bn ($100bn).

So as early as the summer of 1997, while still recovering from the adverse publicity of the *Daily Mail* letter, Gent cuddled up to Ginn. He suggested that they should be "working more closely together" – that Vodafone should buy AirTouch's European business, for which AirTouch would get a large dollop of Vodafone equity. He made his case well and waited for a positive answer, but this was unrequited love. Ginn suggested, politely but firmly, that Gent should get lost.

What happened over the next few years sounds more like a love story than a corporate deal. Ginn's immediate rejection of Gent's approach had less to do with pride flying in the face of strategic good sense and more to do with the possibility that Bell Atlantic would buy AirTouch instead. Bell and AirTouch had worked in joint ventures and seemed to fit well together. The marriage seemed set but Bell had last minute nerves. At the end of this first attempt at a merger, AirTouch was jilted at the altar as Bell put together a merger with GTE, another American telecoms group.

But even before it had digested GTE, Bell was hungry for more such deals. It came back for AirTouch partly as a marriage of convenience. This could make Bell less, rather than more, likely to come under investigation by regulatory authorities. Although the addition of AirTouch to GTE and Bell Atlantic would obviously make the whole entity larger, Bell could at least argue that it now had the making of a competitive powerhouse, able to take on the mighty AT&T. Secondly, there was the question of geography. Bell Atlantic chairman Ivan Seidenberg wanted to use AirTouch to break into the market in the western United States. If the deal with Bell had gone through it would have created a coast-to-coast link-up for the 61 million users in the US and put pressure on AT&T to lower its prices.

There was an important third motive. AirTouch and Bell had a no-competition clause written into their joint venture arrangement. Therefore, as competitors, AirTouch could have forced Bell to sell the GTE mobile businesses it had just inherited through its earlier merger. As part of the same group, however, this would not need to happen.

Everything seemed to make more sense. Certainly, everything made sense to Sam Ginn. As the combined Bell Atlantic/GTE moved in for AirTouch, Ginn knew he was about to move from being wealthy to being filthy rich. At worst, he knew he could walk away from AirTouch with over $142m (nearly £90m) simply from the bonuses due to him, not to mention the share options due to him at Bell Atlantic's bid price of $71 (£45) a share. And when Vodafone's Ken Hydon landed in New York on the instructions of his boss, things became better still.

Hydon's arrival in New York, though dramatic, was hardly a surprise when one looked at the telecoms market at that moment in time. The world's telecommunications industry was buzzing with takeover and merger rumours as bidding intensified for the largest US mobile phone operator. Several other companies were rumoured to be ready with rival bids. One of them was MCI WorldCom, the world's fastest growing telecoms company, although after sniffing around for a short while MCI said it was "currently" not interested in a deal. Bernie Ebbers, MCI WorldCom's colourful head, had considered putting in a rival offer for a week or so but in the end pulled out because, acting somewhat out of character, he believed that the game was simply too rich for him. Maybe Ebbers even then was beginning to understand the mess that he already begun to get himself into.

Nonetheless, it was clear that the bidding war could escalate, given AirTouch's global position. The strategic appeal of AirTouch was such that it would have been surprising had its sale not been appealing to more than just one player. The markets thought that there would be several. Other potential suitors mentioned were British Telecom, Atlanta-based BellSouth Corporation and a fast-emerging German telecoms business known as Mannesmann.

All three groups either described the reports of their interest as "pure rumour and speculation" or declined to comment. There was little doubt, however, that all three were busy in discussions with investors and bankers. Of the three, British Telecom certainly seemed the least likely, as any AirTouch deal would threaten its recent link-up with AT&T, the dominant long-distance carrier in the US. But BT along with all the others enjoyed the boost to its share price.

The share price frenzy was perversely due to the prospect of lower revenues in the future. Around the world telecommunications markets had become more competitive, with sometimes three, four or more companies vying for subscribers. As profit margins fell, it was clear that there would be a consolidation in the industry which would see only large international operators survive. The fight over AirTouch fuelled expectations that particular stocks would bid (or be bid for), and the share prices of telecoms companies increased across the board.

Share prices were going crazy – and Vodafone's own was arguably the craziest of the lot. By January 8, 1999, Vodafone shares were trading on 65 times earnings, compared with an average of 24 for the FTSE 100 index at that time. Nevertheless hard information on any of the deals was scarce; investors and analysts were getting increasingly frustrated. One market watcher remarked "All of the companies share prices were running on vapour." That said, the same people and countless others kept on buying as many telecom shares as they could lay their hands on.

With Gent enjoying his holiday on the other side of the world, Vodafone feigned disinterest to the press. But behind the scenes Hydon and others were playing an enthusiastic brand of hard ball in negotiations with AirTouch. The stakes for Gent and Vodafone could barely be understated. The deal stood to make Vodafone worth at least as much as the ailing former UK telecoms monopoly British Telecom.

After intense negotiations, both in-house and with AirTouch, Vodafone trumped Bell Atlantic's $71 (£45) a share bid with a $86 (£54) a share bid of its own. Suddenly, the San Francisco-based firm was currently facing two offers, one worth $48bn from the largest regional phone company in the US, and another of $55m from Britain's biggest mobile phone operator. Both operations seemed to complement AirTouch's business nicely. Bell Atlantic at the time of the deal had more than 43 million telephone access lines and 10 million wireless customers worldwide. Vodafone had mobile operations in 23 countries, with more than 28 million customers. Its ventures covered a population of nearly 900 million people. It was no wonder that Ginn was all smiles as he watched the bidding war for AirTouch unfold.

Bell Atlantic . . .

A flurry of offers and counter-offers followed. Eventually Vodafone won, but this was by no means the end of the story. Although Bell Atlantic had lost, Seidenberg was an arch-pragmatist. He looked at the mobile businesses Vodafone AirTouch had, looked at his own and thought that there could still be a deal to be done. So it was that September 1999 saw the second of Gent's mega deals. Vodafone AirTouch and the new Bell Atlantic/GTE Corporation combine, undeterred by their earlier clash, had agreed to create a new mobile phone business in the US. The new firm, which brought together Vodafone's US mobile operations with Bell Atlantic Mobile would also drew in the assets of GTE, Bell Atlantic's recent purchase. The new company would have a value of more than $70bn (£43bn) and served around 20 million customers at that time. More significant than any measure of absolute statistics in this era of telephone-number-sized deals, it produced one very, very significant fact. The deal made the new combine, to be called Verizon Wireless, the largest wireless business in the US with coverage of more than 90% of the population.

Vodafone, however, would only be the minority shareholder, with 45% of the business relative to Bell's 55%. The board of the new enterprise would consist of seven members, four nominated by Bell Atlantic and three by Vodafone AirTouch. Furthermore, Seidenberg and Gent were both on the board of the venture. The new board of Verizon Wireless put Denny Strigl in charge of the new venture, a post which he still retains at the time of writing. The president and chief executive, Strigl was an experienced operator. He needed to be, because the task of integrating the domestic wireless operations of Bell Atlantic, Vodafone AirTouch and GTE was likely to be a commercial and political minefield. Strigl had established his reputation as president and CEO of Bell Atlantic Mobile, and group president and CEO of Bell Atlantic Global Wireless which had businesses in 28 states and international investments all over the world. He had been around and knew what he was doing.

In spite of the complexities of integration, there seemed little doubt at the time that this was a smart deal for both sides. Bell Atlantic chairman Ivan Seidenberg still wanted, as he had earlier that same year, to use AirTouch to break into the market in the western United States. He failed, but at least with a joint venture he effectively had the same thing: access to AirTouch's mobile assets to move to a ready-made coast-to-coast network, better able to compete with existing pan-US wireless companies such as AT&T, Sprint PCS Group and Nextel Communications Inc.

The network that Vodafone inherited in its $62bn January takeover of San Francisco's AirTouch covered most of the western states, while Bell's covered most of the east. The deal appeared to make perfect sense for Gent and Vodafone AirTouch as well: Gent desperately wanted to be in the US. He said: "In a market where penetration levels are relatively low but growth looks set to take off, gaining a nationwide footprint with common technology is of paramount importance." True enough, but Gent was always going to struggle, even with the help of his new AirTouch colleagues, to exercise control over the new venture from his base at Newbury in Berkshire. Gent also decided not to introduce the Vodafone brand into the United States. Instead he chose to rely on the Verizon name, which had come from the new name of Verizon Communications chosen when Bell Atlantic and GTE Corporation decided to merge.

Most of all, however, the deal made sense because through a merger with one US company and joint venture with another, Vodafone had been transformed internationally into a global powerhouse with massive clout. Following the agreement with Bell Atlantic/GTE, Vodafone AirTouch suddenly had over 31 million cellular customers worldwide and interests in 24 countries across five continents. To put this in perspective, just before Gent's phone rang at Sydney Cricket Ground in January of that same year, the number of worldwide Vodafone Group customers amounted only to about 10 million. In his deal making, Gent had certainly been looking for the big one, and in the space of little over six months he had found – and got – two.

Mannesmann . . . the beginning

It is said that good things come in threes and Gent had barely had time to shake hands with Seidenberg on the deal when events took his attention back to Europe. The January deal between Vodafone and AirTouch had made a number of other European telecoms companies nervous. One of the them was the German giant Mannesmann, run by Klaus Esser, a man known as Mr Superbrain in the German media. Although this was a characterization that would be taken up with similar enthusiasm by the British press, Mannesmann insiders saw much more to the man than stereotypical Teutonic efficiency. One colleague who worked closely with him for several years says of Esser: "He was a quiet man and definitely not the sort of guy to be talking all of the time. He listened a lot, compared what he heard with what he already knew. Then he quickly worked out what he had learnt and how that changed his view of the world. He wouldn't always volunteer that view, but if you asked him a question you would get a very precise and clear answer. He was straight and direct and those around him appreciated those virtues. We worked very closely together for some time and I sometimes even found it fun to work for him."

Others not so close to him tended to see only the relentless logic of his actions, rather than the care and thought behind strategic decision making. Especially when it came to making a deal, says the same source: "I saw him as a very clever, very smart, very talented. Above all, he was a very talented deal maker."

Back on January 15, 1999 Gent, just returned from his Antipodean adventure, together with his right hand man Julian Horn-Smith, sat down for dinner with Esser and Kurt Kinzius, his managing director at Mannesmann, at the exclusive Pont de la Tour, a restaurant near Tower Bridge with magnificent views over the City. On that day both Vodafone men were literally on the edges of their seats; they were waiting to hear from the United States about whether their bid for AirTouch would trump that from Bell Atlantic.

Although their minds were elsewhere, Esser wanted to know what Vodafone's future objectives were. Until then Vodafone had enjoyed a spirit of more or less friendly co-opetition across Europe, but now both were growing a little too quickly for them to keep out of each other's way. Would Vodafone and Mannesmann still have a relationship, asked Esser, if Vodafone became Vodafone AirTouch?

According to Esser, Gent effectively replied that if Vodafone lost AirTouch, it would need a partner but if Vodafone won, it would not. Before long, Gent and Horn-Smith would be celebrating their new American purchase, but the relationship over the dinner table was already turning sour. As Esser later told the *Sunday Times*: "Ever since, the question in our minds was whether they [Vodafone] would accept somebody like us as being of partner quality, or merely of target quality." However, on the surface the lunch was still convivial, though hostility was never far away. Neither side trusted the other. The question that had been lingering in Esser's mind would soon answered.

Over the following weeks and months he found himself reading a near-continuous flow of media innuendo and rumour that Vodafone would soon prey on its rival almost every time he picked up a newspaper. Klaus Esser wasn't the sort of man to go down without a fight. He had come too far in successfully transforming what had once been a dreadfully unwieldy industrial conglomerate into a powerful mobile operator. Mannesmann's road up to that point had been an very interesting one. At the beginning of the 1990s, the company was a typical example of a German manufacturing giant. Based in the Ruhr, Germany's industrial heartland, it was heavily dependent on the ups and (mostly) downs of the steel market. Yet somehow it had transformed itself into one of Europe's leading telecoms providers at the forefront of a revolution in mobile technology. It had become a very rare company, straddling the old and the new industrial worlds successfully.

The origins of the company are found in an earlier technological revolution, when in 1885 Reinhard and Max Mannesmann invented a way to produce seamless steel tubes. Once they had developed their method commercially, they set up a company and moved from Berlin to Düsseldorf (the German equivalent of Pittsburgh) to get the best from the supply of skilled labour.

The tubes that the Mannesmanns produced were a crucial element of the ongoing industrial revolution, used for everything from oil pipelines to battle tanks. The company was global well before the term became part of common commercial parlance. Factories in Germany exported to Western and Northern Europe, a Welsh Mannesmann factory supplied the British Empire and North America, while works in Austria delivered tubes to Russia, Eastern Europe and the Mediterranean.

In the first half of the twentieth century, Mannesmann was effectively a vertically integrated steel company. It mined the coal to fire its own steel mills, sold the finished steel products and expanded into the production of engineering equipment. It became a major part of the revival of the German economy under the Nazis and was so successful that the Western allies ordered a break-up of the company after the war. Yet although the steel tube, mining and engineering businesses were split up they managed to form a new conglomerate within three years. During this time the business had diversified into other areas, with a string of acquisitions of engineering and automotive firms.

The biggest transformation of the firm, however, began in 1990 when Mannesmann was awarded Germany's first private mobile phone licence, narrowly beating a rival bid from BMW. Within two years, the Mannesmann "D2" network was operational and quickly established itself as the market leader, beating its former monopoly rival Deutsche Telekom. Following this remarkable success, the firm focused its business on four areas – engineering, pipes, automotive and telecommunications – and sold everything else. Before long telecoms was accounting for 70% of company profits. With telecoms the engine room for growth, Mannesmann expanded across Europe through acquisitions and joint ventures. It joined up with Germany's rail network to create Arcor, a landline phone business. It worked with Olivetti in Italy to create the mobile phone network Omnitel and landline operator Infostrada. In France it became a partner of Vivendi. In an echo of Vodafone's activities, the company spent $44bn on acquisitions in 1999 alone. There was no British partner, however, which seemed to be a curious omission.

Mannesmann was seen as a golden stock by investors and managed to survive a financial scandal which claimed the resignation of Werner Dieter, Esser's predecessor. When Esser came on board in place of the ill-fated Dieter, the fortunes of Mannesmann had improved on an accelerating curve. Mannesmann had a further slice of luck when it became the prime beneficiary of Olivetti's victory in its bid for Telecom Italia. To win regulatory clearance for the deal, Olivetti had to sell its existing mobile licence stake in Omnitel and Mannesmann, its junior partner in the deal, bought this up.

Also at the centre of Mannesmann's move into technology was Lars Berg, a Swede who found himself on the board of the German blue chip. He was given responsibility for the telecommunications expansion plan. He had plenty of experience from his time as chief executive and president of Telia. In an interview in April 1999, when specifically asked whether there was any chance of Mannesmann being devoured by the newly merged Vodafone AirTouch Group, Berg stressed the importance of Mannesmann continuing as an independent company, pointing to steady profits, a share price that had grown by 110% in 1998 and a further 40% to that point in 1999. Berg saw no reason to change things around. "That doesn't rule out cooperation with Vodafone AirTouch, however," he said. "It's a complex world. In some markets, we already are partners with Vodafone AirTouch. In others, we are competitors. That's just how it is in today's telecom world."

Cooperation between Vodafone and Mannesmann, as portrayed by Berg, was indeed a fact of the telecoms world. But getting to know someone through joint ventures and alliances didn't always mean getting to like them, and Esser and Gent clearly didn't get on. Esser had suspected Gent's intentions towards Mannesmann for some time.

You couldn't rally blame Esser for thinking like this. It was part of the culture of the late 1990s boom in technology and other CEOs in other telecoms companies felt much the same way. A bid by Vodafone to take-over Mannesmann would have been part of the "buy or be bought" culture. The frenzy of merger activity in the European telecoms industry matched that seen in the US. Gent would have been aware that, even with his US deals in the bag and with 1999 not even over, to be seen to be doing nothing was not an option. Esser knew it too.

The attractiveness of such a company to Vodafone is clear. Although Vodafone had a strong position as the world's largest in terms of subscribers, it didn't dominate Europe, trailing the likes of Telecom Italia. And while it had stakes in markets from Sweden to Greece, most were minority holdings. It also did not control the markets with the most cellular phone subscribers – Italy and Germany.

Mannesmann, however, was Europe's largest private sector phone operator and controlled two of Europe's three largest mobile phone companies. And unlike Vodafone, it owned a controlling stake in most of them. Nearly all of its earnings in telecoms came from the strong growth in mobile networks. Its principle markets in Italy, Germany and France complemented Vodafone's strengths elsewhere in Europe. With Mannesmann acquired, Vodafone would get control of Germany's biggest cellular company, Mannesmann Mobilfunk, and the second-biggest in Italy in Omnitel.

But if Mannesmann was so strong, then why should it have feared a bid from Vodafone, rather than considered the opposite possibility? The answer lay in the structure of the Mannesmann group of companies. Its headquarters were located in the centre of the Ruhr area once dominated by steel and coal. And while Mannesmann had transformed itself into a telecoms force, much of its baggage was still essentially that of a conglomerate. Investors fretted over a pretty basic question: what did mobiles and steel actually have in common?

It was the same question that had been preying on the mind of Esser himself. Esser wanted to break the company up into two separate entities. The idea was that the engineering and automotive divisions would do Mannesmann's old business while telecoms would be a high growth spin-off. In the early autumn of 1999, Mannesmann confirmed that it wanted to sell engineering, which still accounted for 70% of its sales, in a flotation. Ancient and unwieldy tax laws in Germany made it more efficient to float the engineering business instead of the telecoms side.

In anticipation of its new concentrated focus on telecoms, Mannesmann was keen to spend the cash that was about to come its way. The only way to keep predators from the door, reasoned Esser, was to get the first blow in. Esser's eyes were on Orange, Vodafone's British rival; it was the missing piece in Esser's European jigsaw and would show Gent that he could not be messed about.

While Gent was busy concentrating on forging his deal with Bell Atlantic to create Verizon Wireless, Esser had been carefully trying to get key Orange shareholders on board before making the bid. The largest shareholder with a 44% stake in Orange was Hutchison Whampoa, the Hong Kong trading company owned by the billionaire Li Ka-Shing. Esser negotiated at length with Canning Fok, managing director of Hutchison. When negotiations had reached an advanced stage, Fok asked Esser to widen the discussion to bring in Orange chief executive Hans Snook. The three men met and after some initial jousting the deal was in the bag.

Hans Snook, a former hotelier from Canada, had somehow developed the Orange business into one with high brand recognition with customers, even if doing business with those customers wasn't making any money. It was no wonder that Snook was smiling: he was being offered £10m to stay on for six months after the merger and another £5m if he hung around for the following 18 months and helped to integrate Orange and Mannesmann successfully. Although he made it clear that he would have preferred his company to remain independent, Snook was a realist. He told the press conference: "We had come to the conclusion that an acquisition – either by us or of us – had at some point to form part of our strategy. When Mannesmann approached us about 10 days ago they found a meeting of minds." Snook realized that Mannesmann had the firepower to swallow up Orange at a high price without making its bankers blink. So Orange might as well go quietly rather than put up a fight. Mannesmann had to pay dearly for the deal, roughly the equivalent of £5000 for every one of Orange's customers, about twice what Deutsche Telekom had paid for One2One customers earlier in 1999. The deal raised the stakes: Esser had better be right about his high growth projections for the growth of mobile and integrated telephony across Europe.

Esser was confident that he was, and was quickly making arrangements to announce the deal to the world. He was clearly excited at the success of his strategy. And in one sense Mannesmann's sense of strategy was impressive: along with D2, Germany's leading mobile operator and its holding in Cegetel, which owned the SFR consortium in France, the Omnitel deal had almost made Mannesmann's European network complete. The only gap was Britain and now that gap would be filled by Orange. The deal did not require approval from Mannesmann shareholders so Esser thought that he might as well go ahead and announce it.

He knew that rumours about his intentions would somehow reach Gent ahead of any announcement. Gent would soon be on the phone – and he wasn't going to be happy. Esser was right. Gent was at another conference when he heard the whispers that Esser was about to buy Orange. He later recalled: "I contacted him and said 'Here's a better idea. Before you finally commit, why don't we sit down and discuss it?'" But Esser had neither the time nor the inclination to talk – the world was waiting to hear his news and he wasn't about to let them down. So it was that on Thursday October 21, 1999 Esser found himself standing on a press conference podium with Snook, announcing a £20bn deal to the outside world.

Vodafone and Mannesmann had been working very closely in Europe up until that point. In the past they had done so in their mutual interests, as joint partners in Omnitel in Italy and in D2 in Germany. Surely, asked those journalists attending the conference, the deal with Orange changed everything. Suddenly Mannesmann owned the company with which Vodafone was locked in a fierce battle for control of the UK market. Esser denied it: he tried simultaneously to brag about the Orange deal and pretend that nothing much would change the joint ventures that Vodafone and Mannesmann worked upon. Esser acknowledged that the relationship between himself and Gent was not sweetness and light but thought it a price worth paying: "I acknowledge that it makes life in management a little more difficult but in return it also makes life for shareholders a little richer."

The investors, analysts and the media were soon inundating the Vodafone press office. How would Gent react? Wasn't this a humiliating setback for Vodafone? Gent wasn't about to dance to the tune of unsolicited inquiries but in truth he felt humiliated and incandescent with rage. He had himself contributed to the situation by a strategic mistake earlier in the year. Following the deal with AirTouch, Vodafone had, after plenty of heated debate at board room level, decided to sell its 17.5% stake in E-Plus, the third largest German mobile service. In doing this it had put everything into its relationship with Mannesmann. Although the Vodafone board eventually backed the move, not everyone was convinced that this had been a wise move.

A timely study by the analysts Salomon Smith Barney in August 1999 had highlighted weaknesses in the Vodafone strategy. Vodafone arguably needed Mannesmann in a partnership more than Mannesmann needed Vodafone, the study suggested. With Mannesmann, Vodafone would become unbeatable in the European mobile communications market. Without it, the group would be just another British company grappling with the problem of getting the better of a much better placed rival from mainland Europe. The Salomon study warned: "Mannesmann has a mind of its own . . . it has become strong enough to pursue its own strategy independently [of Vodafone]."

Yet in his own mind, Gent believed Esser had double-crossed him, contravening a gentleman's agreement not to compete on each other's territory. Whether or not there was ever such an agreement is open to doubt. If it existed, neither Gent nor Esser regarded each other as gentlemen any longer. Whatever the truth, Vodafone was now firmly caught on the back foot. Although Vodafone, with the newly acquired AirTouch, was much larger overall, Mannesmann's acquisition of Orange made it effectively Europe's largest wireless telecoms company, bigger even than Vodafone's European operations.

For Esser, Vodafone plus AirTouch was a different proposition from Vodafone alone. Vodafone had become a threat, so he bought Orange as a defensive move. For Gent, Mannesmann plus Orange was a different proposition from Mannesmann alone. The new, improved Mannesmann was a threat. The crazy logic of the 1990s technology boom demanded that Gent must now do something to trump Mannesmann's move. And do it quickly.

The Impossible Dream

When Klaus Esser stepped down from the podium after the announcement of Mannesmann's acquisition of Orange, he knew that his life would never be the same again. The sensational news had delighted his colleagues, alarmed his investors – and infuriated Chris Gent.

To his colleagues, Esser had transformed his already strong reputation into one of hero status. All at Mannesmann knew that Esser was in effect staking the future of the company on this one deal. Orange was a large loss-making business whose only real asset was the continued rapid growth of its customer base. The important thing, reasoned Esser, was that the deal sent a strong signal to Vodafone that Mannesmann must not be seen as an acquisition target by the clearly deal-hungry Gent. And for that Esser had the gratitude of his colleagues.

Investors were not quite as convinced as Esser that buying Orange was such a great deal. After coming up with almost £20bn for Snook's company, Esser, as an intelligent man, knew that he was taking something of a gamble. In retrospect the deal seems wildly overpriced, but even at the time, in the height of the telecoms boom, it raised eyebrows. While Esser saw the move as a strategic necessity to maintain the company's independence, the shareholders took a different view. Mannesmann's stock price took a big tumble, falling by 8% on the announcement of the Orange deal. Existing shareholders were left grappling with both the huge dilution of their own holdings and a growing debt mountain. Investors and analysts suddenly began fretting that the Orange deal would hurt the Mannesmann share price permanently.

Esser seemed happy to use his record as the major deterrent to a serious bid from Vodafone and had concluded that "a bid may be difficult for others to do because we have been spoiling our shareholders with enormous returns." He also pointed out that Mannesmann had some existing poison-pill arrangements that that could hinder anyone from making a bid. Because its swift purchase of Orange made it all but impossible for anyone to stop the deal from proceeding, a bidder would have to swallow both – something that would stretch even the likes of Vodafone.

After a few more days of sliding share prices, Esser was asked again whether the Mannesmann share price was starting to look attractive to others. This time he dismissed the possibility of a bid for his company with an irritable wave of his hand, as if trying to swat away a fly, and said tersely: "I don't see any realistic risk of a hostile takeover."

How wrong he was. Gent were fast becoming a master of the deal. Gent's strength, says one of his close colleagues, is his ability to put himself in the other person's shoes when negotiating: "He always has a finely tuned antenna for the motivations of the guy on the other side of the table. He is therefore immensely persuasive." The same could not be said for Esser's antenna. Although Esser could see what was in it for himself and his colleagues, he totally underestimated the importance which Gent had attributed to what he saw as their gentleman's agreement over Orange. It wasn't that Vodafone wanted Orange for itself. Far from it, not least because competition rules would not allow it. It was just that a Mannesmann with a British foothold through Orange represented not only a direct threat but also undermined all Vodafone's existing alliances with Mannesmann across Europe.

Esser's dismissive reaction to the threat of a hostile takeover, although catastrophic, was understandable. Even if Gent was furious (and he was) there seemed too many obstacles to his launching Vodafone's bid for Mannesmann. In 1999 he had already brokered two massive deals, first to merge with AirTouch in the US and then to put all its US mobile assets into a basket with Bell Atlantic and GTE in the Verizon Wireless venture. The second of these deals was only a few weeks old and Esser reasoned that, with so much on his plate, Gent surely wouldn't have the stomach – or even the time – for another large acquisition, even in his own European backyard.

Esser and Gent hadn't really clicked back in the Pont de la Tour at their meeting in January, on the day that Vodafone had closed in on the merger with AirTouch. And what Esser failed to understand was the scale of Gent's stamina and ambition. Far from being weary after two big deals in the US, he was spoiling to enter the fray. Initially, Gent had been hoping to cajole Esser into a friendly merger but with Mannesmann's hand declared over Orange, that had become unlikely.

Esser was not alone in underestimating Gent's determination. Many analysts claimed that Mannesmann was likely to be out of the price range of potential buyers, including Vodafone AirTouch. And it wasn't as if Vodafone would be the only buyer in the market. France Telecom had just bought control of Germany's third largest network, E-Plus, from Vodafone, while at the time Deutsche Telekom was thought to have an eye on France's Buoygues Telecom. Neither was thought big enough to take on the razor-sharp Esser and Mannesmann; nor were the lumbering British former monopoly BT nor the ill-fated MCI WorldCom. BT, for the moment at least, was content to sit on the sidelines: it didn't like the Mannesmann move, but couldn't see any advantage in intervention. MCI WorldCom chose not to intervene, although it remained a threat – in the heady days of the technology boom at least.

Furthermore, it was thought that Vodafone would also face difficulties in mounting a hostile bid in Germany, where competition law was hostile to foreign takeovers. Times were changing: Olivetti's daring bid earlier in 1999 for Telecom Italia had broken down barriers there and many felt that Fortress Germany could one day crumble. Yet no company to that date had ever succeeded with a hostile takeover bid in Germany. While in the past German companies were especially active in the purchase of foreign firms, the reverse had not applied. German firms, with their intricate mesh of company shares and executive mandates, also ensured that the parent company in Germany retained overall control of the enterprise, even when the majority of shares were in foreign ownership. In addition, German corporate law gave small shareholders extensive rights, thereby making takeovers by foreign companies especially difficult.

The omens for Gent were not good, to put it mildly. Until Vodafone's bid for Mannesmann, the previous largest British bid for a German company was an agreed takeover of a polymer company at a modest £280m, an amount nearly 300 times smaller than the sum that Gent would soon be proposing. And the Vodafone takeover of Mannesmann was anything but agreed. To most observers in Germany, the thought of having one of its largest companies taken over by foreigners was unthinkable. To many outside the Fatherland it seemed like an impossible dream.

Gent was one of the few who believed that a bid for Mannesmann would be difficult but by no means impossible. Once he had learnt of Mannes-mann's bid for Orange, he had been taking daily soundings from investors to establish at what price they would back a Vodafone takeover bid for Mannesmann. At this stage, Gent and his team were desperate not to get carried away. Esser had seen the Mannesmann share price slide because investors did not share his optimism on the wisdom of purchasing Orange. That had brought Mannesmann into play but the potential bid was a massive one. On the one hand, it had to be high enough to make Mannesmann investors think that Vodafone was making a serious offer. On the other hand, Gent was acutely aware that the bid couldn't be so high that Vodafone's own share price would implode as a result. In the world of inflated telecoms takeovers at that time, it was not inconceivable that a deflated Vodafone share price could follow a mispitched bid and that Vodafone itself could become of interest to other parties.

Gent was also acutely aware that if he couldn't negotiate an agreed takeover with Esser then this would be the first hostile bid that he and Vodafone had ever made. In spite of his reputation as some sort of daring corporate raider, Gent's real skill lay in the art of negotiation rather than confrontation. He had shown supreme diplomatic skills in winning control of AirTouch, somehow without incurring the wrath of Bell Atlantic, AirTouch's other suitor. A little over six months later, his relations with its boss Ivan Seidenberg were so warm that he had managed to persuade Bell Atlantic into the Verizon Wireless joint venture. Charm and guile were Gent's strengths rather than hostility and trench warfare.

For a combination of the reasons given, Esser seemed convinced that Vodafone would make no bid. Even if it did, he reasoned, Mannesmann shareholders would overwhelmingly stay loyal to the team that had delivered great returns on their investment for several years. Others in Esser's press office were far less sure that a serious battle would not break out. One senior former Mannesmann press officer recalls: "In the Mannesmann head office there were always a lot of rumours about mergers, takeovers and other deals. Up until the Orange deal we were fending off inquiries about a friendly merger with Vodafone. As it later turned out Gent and Esser had talked about this at various stages. But to put it in perspective, we also heard rumours about interest from our sources at BT and AT&T and a few others."

After Mannesmann's deal with Orange, however, the Mannesmann press office was swamped by a large number of strange phone calls from the media about a possible hostile Vodafone bid. At the time these were described officially by a Mannesmann spokesman as "dubious rumours" but the same spokesman now admits that "while we expected a number of calls from journalists, we were surprised by the volume. Furthermore, some calls seemed to have a very specific knowledge of aspects of Vodafone/Mannesmann joint ventures and the form which a possible bid might take. We could only assume that they had been speaking to Vodafone people and knew something we didn't."

Battle begins

The spokesman's fears were soon realized. When the first bid came, it valued Mannesmann plus Orange at £68 bn. Once his mind had been made up, Gent had moved with near lightning speed. Colleagues of Gent all point to quick decision making as one of his major strengths. Warren Finegold, a UBS Warburg banker who worked on the bid says: "We had to put together the offer for Mannesmann in a matter of days. That's incredibly fast in this business." But speed was fast becoming Gent's trademark. He even flew to Düsseldorf to propose a takeover formally. In making the bid he made it sound like the natural consequence of a long love affair, rather than the wrath of a lover scorned. The businesses of Mannesmann and Vodafone AirTouch, he said "belong together for many years and are natural partners in Europe".

Esser, however, clearly didn't see it like that. Another of Esser's aides in the Mannesmann investor relations department recalls how his attitude hardened on the day the bid was announced. From now on, the everyday course of the business took second place to the battle to keep Mannesmann as an independent force. There was only one battle to fight now and that was for survival. "From that day, my job and life completely changed for several months. I was working only on this project. The survival of the business as an independent concern came at the expense of everything else. Preparing the marketing against the bid, doing roadshows and talking to every investor we could took up every single minute of my already long working day."

The takeover, said Gent, would create an unmatched European mobile network, a global brand. The result would be a colossal company, with mobile phone interests in 15 European countries – with 30 million customers in that continent alone – and 28 countries and 42 million customers worldwide. Vodafone said the merger would generate savings of more than £1bn by 2004 and that there would be no redundancies.

How it is possible to generate such a level of savings without redundancy is puzzling until one realizes that the redundancies would be moved onto a third party. Savings would be generated by selling off parts of the Mannesmann business. Gent wanted the fast-moving parts of the Mannesmann empire, but he had no intention of turning Vodafone into an industrial conglomerate. His plan at the start, like Esser's, was that Vodafone would seek to split off Mannesmann's engineering and automotive operations into a separate company. What the purchasers of these operations did then about redundancies was entirely up to them. Esser had already reached the same conclusion. Mannesmann's executive committee had already given approval for his plan to cut its stake in the engineering/automotive unit to under 50%. And when Gent announced the Vodafone bid, Mannesmann brought forward its plans to split up the company to the middle of 2000, one year earlier than previously planned.

To many casual observers, therefore, the ambitions of both Gent and Esser for Mannesmann seemed essentially the same. Both would involve splitting the group into two; both would eventually sell off the slower-growth parts of the business; and both would require high levels of redundancy, albeit after a change of ownership. Yet in other ways their strategy was very different. Vodafone sought to concentrate on a purely mobile strategy, but Esser and Mannesmann favoured an integrated strategy for telecommunications. Esser wanted mobiles to be part of an offering alongside cable, broadband and the internet. He didn't want to rely too much on mobile, no matter how fast that market was growing as 1999 drew to a close. He feared that the market for mobile phones would soon reach its limit and wanted a wider base for growth. Esser's aide in investor relations confirms this: "Klaus believed in his vision with a real passion. He saw an integrated company with integrated products for their clients, but Vodafone believed only in the mobile industry." There were other differences as well. "Mannesmann wanted to have majority holdings in its company, especially in Europe, whereas Vodafone's holdings were in minority stakes."

A pro-Mannesmann investment banker summed up those differences: "Of the really big markets in Europe, Mannesmann controlled its German and Italian operations and had a stronger influence in France. Vodafone only controlled the UK. Vodafone's minority positions in continental Europe's main markets made it look a bit like an investment trust." Outside Europe, Vodafone had lots of minority holdings in other companies worldwide. It had investments in the Far East and the US where Mannesmann had nothing at all. The aide saw this as a major weakness for Mannesmann to exploit: "Part of our marketing strategy was to say we want quality stakes, we want majority stakes in the whole thing rather than low quality minority stakes in the telecoms business of the Seychelles."

Gent's first bid was rejected out of hand by Esser almost before it had been made. Although the Mannesmann board was not due to discuss the bid until its regular meeting the following Friday, Esser made a tetchy announcement on Sunday November 14, 1999 which effectively described the offer as an insult to Mannesmann shareholders. It was clear how Esser felt and in the context of the technology boom, if not in retrospect, he seemed to have a point. Even though it is now difficult to see how £65bn can be an undervalution of anything, the first offer did seem to most observers to undervalue Mannesmann by some margin.

The rejection of the bid did not surprise Gent in the slightest. But the derisive reaction of Esser and his colleagues to the Vodafone bid really rattled him. At a conference at London's Savoy Hotel on the following Tuesday, his answers to reporters' questions were as full of venom and contempt for his German rival as the latter's had been for him two days earlier.

Gent's responses made it clear that while he had taken earlier merger talk between the two at the Pont de la Tour – and subsequently – seriously, Esser had not. As Gent put it, his voice brimming with sarcasm: "We had put it to Mannesmann that we would like to put the assets together, but only when they were ready to do so. Dr Esser didn't like the idea, but he never said so." The talks had effectively been a smokescreen behind which Esser was looking to double-cross Gent over Orange. This was all a far cry from the briefing that Gent had given nearly six months earlier at the same hotel. At that time, a relaxed Gent told journalists that he had no designs on Mannesmann. In fact, he countered, if anyone ever tried to pick on Mannesmann, he "would be there to help *them*" (author's italics).

Even in the high-octane world of technology acquisitions, no one doubted that by "them" Gent had meant helping Mannesmann, rather than the aggressor it faced. But now it was clear, following the Orange deal, that Gent would cheerfully help anybody else with designs on putting the boot in. In a terse voice, he told the business journalists present: "We have studied this very closely and we believe that an unsolicited takeover can be achieved."

Within a week the bid was increased. Its timing was mischievous in the extreme: it came at 7 a.m. on Friday November 19, two hours before the Mannesmann board was due to meet at its Ruhr headquarters to discuss the first offer on a formal basis. For several hours earlier that morning and on the previous day, Mannesmann directors had been locked in intense conversation with its investment banking teams of Morgan Stanley and Merrill Lynch. The directors emerged ready to reject the original bid at their formal board meeting only to find a second bid on the table and hundreds of man-hours wasted considering one that was now irrelevant. The irritated Mannesmann directors chose to delay discussion of the second bid until the following week.

When they did, they found that Vodafone had upped their offer to €124bn (£79bn), an all paper offer of €240 per Mannesmann share, and a sizeable premium to shareholders. The sheer size of the bid was no less breath-taking when written about now than three years ago, perhaps even more so. It was bigger than the $122bn (£77bn) friendly acquisition of Sprint by the American telecoms giant MCI WorldCom. It was also four times the size of the bid by the Bank of Scotland for NatWest – the previous largest hostile bid by a British company. By every yardstick imaginable, this proposed takeover was in a completely different league.

On Sunday November 28, the 20-member supervisory board of the

German firm met in Düsseldorf again and rejected the revised bid. A substantially improved offer was on the table, so the hostility of Mannesmann to this second bid took many by surprise. The bid, said the company in an official statement, did not contain a cash element and was unattractive to shareholders. "Furthermore, Mannesmann does not consider a combination with Vodafone AirTouch as strategically attractive," it added brusquely.

The hostile bid

Gent now knew that all hope of an agreed takeover had disappeared. His less favoured option of a hostile bid was looming large, and it was something he was prepared to do if necessary. The battle was already descending into a personal one between Esser and Gent. The struggle for shareholder support now involved each CEO attacking the other's credibility, with Gent getting personal more often than not. "Esser is intent on securing hero status as the man who transforms Mannesmann into a European national telecommunications champion," he said in an interview with *Sunday Business*. "This guy simply does not want to talk to us; it is quite incredible."

Whatever the level of personal hostility, both parties knew that the clock had started ticking. In a proposed hostile takeover, Vodafone was now obliged to send its offer document to shareholders by mid-December, starting the 60-day takeover period, with the final closing date of the offer at around mid-February 2000. By then, Gent hoped, it would have won over 50% of Mannesmann investors.

There were regulatory obstacles to overcome. Vodafone knew that Orange would have to be demerged to avoid competition problems in the event of a successful takeover. The issue produced an ugly showdown. Esser had already feared that Gent would not take his bid for Orange lying down and so had tried to secure a guarantee from Goldman Sachs, which had also advised Li Ka-Shing at Hutchison Whampoa on Orange, that it would not act for Vodafone in a hostile bid. Mannesmann had complained that the bankers had access to confidential information about the group's financial state, having acted for the group in the past. But a High Court judge dismissed Mannesmann's ploy in the most damning terms and Goldman Sachs was allowed to work with Vodafone.

Once the revised bid had been launched and the squabbles over who was to represent who had been sorted out, Esser began an all-out media charm offensive to try to convince his shareholders that they should reject the bid. "I'm feeling good about the situation for two reasons," he told the *Sunday Telegraph*. "One, because it is about hot competition. And the other because I think this is a situation we're about to win." The message from Esser continued in that week's *Der Spiegel* magazine: "The growth prospects of the group are gigantic. . . . Data business via mobile phones will give us a new thrust." According to those close to him at the time, this was not just public bravado. "Esser wasn't just talking confident. He really was that confident. And so were the rest of us," said one.

German politicians, the media and the unions also gave cause for confidence. Gent knew that a hostile bid for Mannesmann would unleash a huge wave of negative sentiment in Germany and he had tried in vain to calm the nationalistic furore. "I realize we may be stirring up national sensibilities with this offer, but quite honestly, I think that it should be decided on the basis of value, not emotion and certainly not politics," he told *Sunday Business*.

Fat chance. In fact, politicians were already getting involved, in large numbers and at lots of different levels. At the European level, commissioners were throwing their weight around. The European commissioner for Enterprise, Erkki Liikanen, said pointedly "our competition authorities will not allow markets to centralize in ways that do not benefit consumers," when asked about the bid. Competition commissioner Mario Monti, meanwhile, used the takeover bid to further his own agenda for pan-European takeover rules. He was backed by the German Minister of Finance, Hans Eichel, who called for new competition rules in Europe in order to "avoid a culture clash between Anglo-American capitalism and the consensual German model".

The German Chancellor Gerhard Schröder had plenty to say – to start with at least. Reported as being "very disturbed" by the news of the proposed takeover, Schröder came out and claimed that "hostile takeovers destroy a company's culture". The remarks upset the British Prime Minister Tony Blair, who in public had described the takeover battle as a "purely commercial matter". Blair pulled Schröder to one side at a summit meeting in Florence and asked his German colleague to tone down his rhetoric. Schröder, stung by Blair's private rebuke and also by criticism from the German business community, said little else of note during the protracted takeover process.

Other German politicians didn't hold back. The Minister President of the state of North Rhine Westphalia, Wolfgang Clement, spoke out strongly against the hostile takeover. Clearly pandering to nationalist sentiment, Clement declared that Mannesmann should not become the "filial of a London company". He accused Vodafone of "playing Monopoly with the Mannesmann company against the interests of the employees, the works councillors, the management and the supervisory board". Jürgen Rüttgers, Clement's CDU rival in the approaching state elections, attempted to match his outrage, stating that "a company broken up and thousands of jobs destroyed merely to ensure short-term profits for international investors" would not be tolerated. While German business, on the whole, adopted a less interventionist tone than the politicians, Hans Peter Stihl, the president of the German Chamber for Trade and Industry, demanded a law to prevent "thoroughly fit, competitively successful enterprises from being misappropriated with parts of the company being disposed of to those who offer most".

More conciliatory were the views expressed by Ludolf-Georg von Wartenberg, general secretary of the Confederation of German Industries. Von Wartenberg argued that politicians should not influence the Vodafone–Mannesmann battle but leave it to the decisions of the economic participants. Professor Klandt of the European Business School in Mainz said that most of Germany's business community saw hostile takeovers as socially unacceptable. "We potentially will have a problem in this area. Many German managers will not be very happy. I think it's part of the game and it's not possible to avoid this kind of behaviour."

The unions were predictably the most vociferous of those against the takeover. Klaus Zwickel, the chairman of the powerful IG Metall trade union, who personally sat on the Mannesmann board, was particularly angry: "European business culture, characterized by joint consultation [with the unions], must not be destroyed by hostile takeovers." Zwickel was listening to the fears of the workers: the Mannesmann workforce was predictably horrified at the prospect of a takeover by Vodafone. Representatives from IG Metall and the Mannesmann group works council immediately rejected Vodafone's bid as unacceptable. The chairman of the company's shop stewards committee, Jürgen Ladberg, declared that the Mannesmann workforce "would do everything it could to prevent a takeover". A few days earlier the works council had organized a 10-minute token strike in several Mannesmann companies and employees demonstrated again against the takeover on Monday, November 22.

The following day over 1,000 union representatives for the company in Düsseldorf met to discuss further action. Zwickel declared that everyone associated with Mannesmann "wanted this attempt to fail". He criticized Vodafone for only being interested in Mannesmann's mobile phone business so that they could "throw a bothersome competitor out of the market". He described Vodafone's behaviour as "brutal" and an "expression of predator capitalism which aims only at short- term profits for the shareholders". He said that Vodafone was interested only in cutting the "best fillet" out of Mannesmann.

Zwickel and Ladberg both believed that the Mannesmann vision for the future to be far more attractive for shareholders, workers and customers, because it was focused on integration of fixed line, mobile phone and internet operations. At the end of the meeting, a so-called "Declaration of Düsseldorf" was adopted in which the Mannesmann works councillors expressed their united resistance to a takeover by Vodafone: "We are strongly against the previous and all possible future attempts for a hostile takeover of the Mannesmann Corporation through Vodafone AirTouch or any other bidder. We see the attempt at a hostile takeover as a flagrant disregard of our company culture which is based on a broad participation of employees and their trade unions in all major company decisions."

Claus Eilrich, IG Metall's spokesman, claimed that the hostile takeover by Vodafone threatened the consensual business culture which has been the key to Mannesmann's success. He told the BBC on January 14: "In principle we've nothing against foreign companies taking stakes in German firms. What we don't like, and what we fear from Vodafone's actions, is that the business culture which has been developed over years at Mannesmann – which takes account of the interests of workers as well as shareholders – will be destroyed by a Vodafone takeover."

Gent had expected a bad reaction from Mannesmann workers and their union representatives, but the extent of their ferocity alarmed him. So he set to work to overcome the workers' opposition by presenting a more employee-friendly image. On November 24, he personally penned an "open letter to the employees of Mannesmann" and placed it in all leading German daily newspapers. The letter made several points. Firstly, that the merger of Mannesmann and Vodafone AirTouch would not mean any additional job losses. Secondly, that the rights of the employees, trade unions and works councillors would be more fully recognized. Mannesmann AG would continue to have a "co-determined" supervisory board with employee representatives. Thirdly, that employment prospects in telecoms would be improved in favour of the Düsseldorf region.

While the support of German politicians, the unions and some business leaders was clearly helpful, Esser found the nationalistic overtones both embarrassing and detrimental to Mannesmann's cause. He told *Der Spiegel* magazine: "At the moment national pathos is of no help to us. This does not correspond to the strategy of Mannesmann. We are building a pan-European company with the focus on European customers and markets, and we are battling at present for the trust of international investors."

Esser had good reason to fret over the impact of nationalistic sentiment on international investors. The irony was that Mannesmann's share register was unusual for a German company. According to one set of figures, 70% of the shares after the Orange deal were be held outside Germany, with Hutchison Whampoa the largest single holder with 10%. Other Mannesmann holders included Anglo-American-owned fund managers, such as Capital, Alliance, Fidelity, Putnam and Mercury Asset Management. Mannesmann, however, while realizing that more of its shareholders than not lay outside German borders, was not above a little nationalistic posturing when it suited it. The company said that its shareholder capital in Germany was solidly behind it and that it would only need to win over a few foreign shareholders to get over the 50% winning line.

Analysts, the conduit of information to many investors, were certainly watching with interest. The outcome of the takeover battle seemed finely balanced. A Reuters survey of analysts in Germany and Britain on the Friday suggested that Vodafone had a 60% chance of success. Those who doubted the wisdom of a Vodafone bid suggested that Esser was right about the better growth potential of his integrated strategy. The projected increase in Mannesmann's data business via mobile phones could have meant the group's value was far higher than Vodafone's revised offer – one of the main points Esser was presenting to investors.

Indeed, the outcome was far from clear. What was clear though, as November neared its end, was that Gent and Vodafone seemed to be fighting not just a company but most of German public opinion. His dream no longer seemed impossible, but still a touch improbable to many who were in a good position to know. Esser had inspired his colleagues with his daring purchase of Orange and now he was inspiring them again as the battle for Mannesmann was joined in earnest. As one of Esser's close aides puts it: "We all believed totally that Mannesmann staying independent was by far and away the best possible solution. And, for a while at least, we all believed totally that Vodafone could not and would not win. Klaus gave us that confidence."

Blood and Betrayal

Although the battle for control of Mannesmann only officially came to life when the group's supervisory board rejected Vodafone's second offer of £79bn, in truth the race for shareholder support had been going on for some weeks. On Tuesday November 23, Mannesmann was able to boast of an early success in its efforts to fend off the hostile bid. The source was hardly a surprise: Hutchison Whampoa owned 10% of Mannesmann and had been instrumental in brokering the deal which saw Orange delivered safely into Klaus Esser's hands. Nevertheless, the news was a timely fillip to Mannesmann staff as Hutchison managing director Canning Fok declared: "Jointly with Orange, Mannesmann will be an outstanding company and better positioned than Vodafone for future opportunities in the telecoms business. The combination of Orange and Mannesmann is, in my opinion, very powerful and offers the best opportunity for Hutchison's shareholders."

The next day saw another victory for Mannesmann. The US AFL-CIO (the American Federation of Labor and Congress of Industrial Organizations), which controlled 13% of the company, directed its pension fund not to accept the offer. The union said that as far as it was concerned the Mannesmann way was the only way. The president of the AFL-CIO, John Sweeney, revealed that the investment managers of the fund had been instructed to oppose Vodafone's bid because "the managers of worker capital have a responsibility to invest those funds in the long term interests of their beneficiaries. [We] believe value is created over the long-term by partnerships among all a corporation's constituents – workers, investors, customers, suppliers and communities. Mannesmann, and the European model of corporate governance under which it is structured, has allowed just those kinds of value-creating partnerships to flourish." In a thoughtful statement, Bill Paterson, director of the AFL-CIO's office of investment, added: "The decision is not just about a takeover, it contains a basic issue. It's about the question of which creates greater long-term value for shareholders, the Anglo-American or the European model. We believe that the European model, which seeks consensus between workers and employers, is the more successful model."

In just 24 hours, Esser had bagged nearly a quarter of the available shares in support of keeping Mannesmann independent. The support of these two shareholders had given him a major boost and, perhaps, the necessary momentum to see off Gent and Vodafone. One Esser aide says: "We never thought it would be easy. We'd expected support from Hutchison and the union movement in America but when it came it was still nice to know that we had a head start. We knew that after that it would still not be easy, but it did make us more confident." Gent's team, meanwhile, saw Mannesmann race into an early lead, but felt the losses had simply flushed out the time-wasters. Now the race was on to win the hearts, minds and wallets of the rest.

After Mannesmann's rejection of the second bid on Sunday November 28, both Esser and Gent kicked off separate multi-city tours in an effort to woo undecided Mannesmann shareholders. Esser began his tour of 20 cities in Gent's backyard of the City of London. In one meeting there with key shareholders he outlined the essentials of his case for keeping Mannesmann independent.

Vodafone, he argued, was the wrong strategy at the wrong price, made in the wrong way. "The value of Mannesmann is significantly higher than the offer on the table," he said. He also claimed that Vodafone's business strategy was changing every few days: "[Vodafone] is looking for a solution to solve their strategy crisis. That is good for them, but not good for Mannesmann. The two portfolios just do not fit. From here on it's simple mathematics. If the shareholders want to get richer, they will get richer with us and our integrated strategy."

Esser had played a smart game with the press, but dealing with investors was a different matter. All the media had wanted were sound bites and snapshots, but investors needed to hear lots of detail and sound reasoning. Under their close questioning, the first cracks in Esser's previously unyieldingly hostile attitude to the Vodafone bid began to emerge. Esser admitted that he would not necessarily keep the door closed on Vodafone forever if the price was right. There is a point "at which a price is very convincing" he admitted. Any chief executive who refused to countenance even an irresistible bid offer would probably find himself dumped by investors pretty quickly.

Esser, however, doubted whether Vodafone would offer such a satisfactory price. One analyst who attended the briefing had his doubts about what the Mannesmann chief was saying: "They have an interesting case, but by no means a compelling one. The question I always come back to is: what can be enhanced that Mannesmann can do by themselves which cannot be enhanced if they do it with Vodafone?"

Gent, meanwhile, was starting his own whistlestop campaign and he seemed to be faring a little better. Within a few days he claimed to have already spoken to around a quarter of Mannesmann shareholders. It had become clear, he claimed, that a great many of them were prepared to swap shares in Mannesmann for Vodafone. A key element of the story of the battle for Mannesmann is founded in the personality and drive of Chris Gent. His first marriage had foundered for a number of reasons, one of which was his capacity to work long hours. Now he had a second wife and a young family, and genuinely came to resent the impact of the travelling he had committed himself to on his personal life. Yet Gent put himself through several gruelling weeks of shareholder meetings all over the world because he knew that a personal appearance from him could sway wavering support. Gent made sure that he attended as many of the 350 roadshow events across the US, UK and mainland Europe as time would allow. John Hahn, a former Morgan Stanley Dean Witter & Co. banker who represented Mannesmann in its defence against Vodafone, admitted that "the guy was on the road constantly".

According to one of Gent's colleagues, this was a crucial factor: "Mannesmann did loads of roadshow presentations but we did even more. And more importantly, Chris always seemed to be there when we needed him most." The Mannesmann investor relations manager confirms the importance of Gent's efforts: "Yes it's true. We did a number of roadshows where we went with another board member rather than Klaus Esser. The investors we saw would then turn around and say "Yesterday we saw Chris Gent personally and now you're only giving us someone who's not Klaus Esser. We want to see him.' Sadly, however, Klaus didn't always have time to see every single investor personally. And yes, that did make a difference in the end."

Many of the roadshows took place during an exhaustive tour of the United States, where many of the investors were based. The Mannesmann investor relations manager says: "We met every single significant investor – and there were hundreds. In the US, we had everything from one-on-one meetings through to large group meetings where we had 50 to

60 together. In all in the US we saw about 150 big investors. By the end we should have known the answer to every single question." Yet there were one or two questions that the Mannesmann team struggled to get to grips with. This manager admits that: "In the US it was always difficult to explain why a combined Mannesmann–Vodafone company with a global reach would not make sense at that time. In those days everyone was thinking how important global reach was. Investors kept saying 'Come on, guys, the fit is perfect geographically, so why don't you want this to happen?' We had to concede that geography was not on our side, but that our integrated product offering was much better than Vodafone's mobile-only set up. In retrospect, I don't think that they really wanted to understand."

With two helter-skelter US tours in progress, it was also inevitable that the two sides would bump into each other from time to time. Sometimes this bordered on the farcical. For those who endured the tours on both sides, a few incidents stood out. Gent and Esser were apparently in New York on the same morning attending consecutive meetings with the same key shareholder. After his meeting, which overran, Gent was shown out via the stairs at the back of the boardroom, just as Esser and his entourage arrived on the same floor in the elevator. There then followed a stilted five-minute period of small talk between Esser and the investor as the investor's secretary scrambled around the boardroom table removing all the Vodafone literature. Only then was Esser allowed in.

There were other moments. Once, when a Mannesmann executive was hailing a cab to leave an investor's headquarters he was startled to find that the same cab was setting down passengers from Vodafone who were going into the same building. On another occasion, a Mannesmann execu-tive was leaving a key investor meeting via an elevator. The elevator door opened and inside was one of his opposite numbers from Vodafone, whom he recognized from their time together on a European joint venture. After several seconds of awkward silence, the Vodafone executive ventured "Are you going up?" to which the Mannesmann man replied "No, we're going down." "I know you are" said the Vodafone man, "but what about the elevator?"

At the end of all the tours, it was difficult for anyone to really see what had been achieved. Most investors didn't need to make their minds up until February so they didn't. Says the Mannesmann aide: "There were a lot of roadshows going on all over the place between November and January but we didn't really see a huge shift in support either way over that time. Investors were really undecided and didn't see any need to rush. They shook our hands, said 'thank you very much' and didn't commit themselves one way or the other. Some investors were very straight with us and said 'look, we think you've got the right strategy and we're going to back you', but the vast majority didn't go that far. They said 'we understand your strategy and we think it makes sense, but we have to wait, make up our minds' and so on. It made it very difficult to predict the outcome and even now I really believe that at least 50% of votes were undecided to some degree right up until the last minute."

Klaus Esser, though, perhaps sensing that the ground was starting to slip from beneath him, stepped up the war of words. On December 8, he declared that shareholders would be "stupid" to accept Vodafone's offer. Speaking at a press conference he pointed out that while Vodafone was growing rapidly, Mannesmann was growing at an even faster rate. "The Mannesmann shareholder has more than 30% growth in store and Vodafone can show a growth rate of 18%. 18% is strong, fair enough. But 30% is much higher," he added, perhaps a little unnecessarily.

Then, however, came another crack in the Esser bravado. He added: "This is not to say that going together is excluded. But we should only do it if it makes sense for our shareholders and if the price is right." But this time he set out his idea of what the price would be. Esser suggested that Mannesmann shareholders deserved at least €300 to €350 per share, as opposed to the €240 being offered.

Big corporate shareholders had been largely unaffected in their deliberations by the popular sentiment in German against Vodafone's bid. But it was different for the retail shareholders. The Mannesmann investor relations manager admits: "The German newspapers probably did impact on retail shareholders. The retail shareholders, however, were a small minority of the whole picture. At the start of the whole process they constituted little more than 10%, but by the end it went down because small shareholders were selling shares to the big guys as the share price went up and up and up."

Nevertheless, who the remaining small shareholders favoured could make all the difference in what seemed likely to be a tight race. Both sides knew it and, on Esser's command, the Mannesmann publicity machine swung into full action. Mannesmann took out full-page advertisements in German newspapers, with a graph showing an 805% rise in its share price since November 1994 and the words "CARRY ON . . ." Vodafone also tried to appeal to the retail shareholder. Newspaper reports suggested that Vodafone spent £10m on an advertising blitz along the lines of the old British Gas "Tell Sid" privatization campaign, although Vodafone sources say that the sum was actually well below this figure.

The retail element of the Mannesmann shareholding really came into focus when one side came a cropper. As Christmas and New Year approached and with most presentations made, Gent felt as though he was in the box seat. So he decided to take a short break and headed down to Cape Town to watch a Test match between England and South Africa just into the New Year. It was here, at least in the eyes of the media, that he committed his only real blunder of the whole Mannesmann takeover bid.

Having invited guests in to the Vodafone corporate box to watch the match, he seemed jovial as he knocked back a few beers. He told one of his guests: "I can't imagine Klaus Esser relaxing here, can you? He's more into German poetry and chess." And then, disastrously, he chose to adopt a Basil Fawlty-style poor German accent and attempted to impersonate his rival: "I haf skied a bit, I haf read zum German poetry and tried to fend off ze hostile takeover." The remarks, though meant as a gentle piece of mickey-taking of his opponent, somehow reached both the British and German newspapers. It caused offence to some German investors and gave the media a stick marked "xenophobia" with which to beat Gent.

Sadly less attention was given at the time to other remarks by Gent at the same time which were to prove remarkably perceptive: "This guy [Esser] is going to go down swinging rather than anything else . . . I think he will try and pull a rabbit out of the hat. But I do not get the impression that they are enjoying this as much as we are."

Esser certainly was worried by the way that the battle was shaping up. Many investors seemed sympathetic but non-committal. Esser suspected that his underlying support was soft. He might, potentially, have a rabbit to pull out of his hat and it would very large one indeed. But first of all he sought to create a smokescreen of confusion and doubt behind which to mask his real intentions. The Mannesmann press office played up the pitfalls that the Vodafone bid could soon encounter. The European Commission was looking at length into the bid. By February 7, when Vodafone's offer was due to close, Brussels was also due to make clear whether a "second phase" investigation, expected to last four months, would be undertaken. While Vodafone officials were supremely confident that no such inquiry would take place, the sheer size of the bid and the issues involved made it easy for Esser to play up the possibility that such an investigation would take place.

He made the most of his chance. "For six to ten months the shares will be in limbo. The strategy grinds to a standstill but in Europe a lot of hot things are going on. Big deals are being made and we sit in the deep freeze . . . those who are not in action now, who see and use the opportunities of the next couple of months, will probably lose the picture." The choice of language, of course, suited Esser very nicely. The prospect of a long period of confusion and paralysis should Vodafone win was clearly designed to make the prospect of a Vodafone bid as unappealing as possible. Other suggestions flew about at the same time. There were complex technical arguments that Vodafone actually needed to win 75% of Mannesmann shares to win effective control of the company, that Vodafone would be required to pay an extra €60bn as a cash sweetener to gain full control of the company and that some shareholders would face higher tax bills if Vodafone bought their shares. Gent was furious at what he saw as Mannesmann's attempt to mislead its shareholders, and pointed out that "none of these issues affect the real choice Mannesmann shareholders have to make".

While Gent was confident that Vodafone was now on the winning path, he also knew that its image was taking a battering in Germany among the politicians, unions and the general public. Even if he won the bid, he would need their goodwill in the longer term. So, on January 20, he agreed to what seemed a modest increase in the offer. Gent would accept Mannesmann owning up to 49% of the merged company – 2% more than previously – but only if the German company dropped its defences. He was also now willing to make concessions on strategic and management

issues and was "prepared to talk about a merger of equals on the management team" – thereby offering Esser and his senior Mannesmann
colleagues the prospect of a job if the deal was completed successfully.
Esser took little notice of what was going on. He was still hoping for his
large rabbit. And how he came within an ace of producing it is one of the
most interesting stories in the battle for control of Mannesmann.

Esser's rabbit

No one really knew precisely what Esser was up to, although there had
been plenty of media speculation that his only major hope was to enlist
the help of a "white knight". Some commentators speculated that Esser
had considered merging Mannesmann's telecoms operations with the
French conglomerate Vivendi in an effort to fend off Vodafone's bid.

Esser was adamant, in public at least, that he would do no such thing. But
by January 2000, Vivendi was refusing to comment on reports that it could
step in as a white knight. And although repeatedly stating that the company wanted to remain independent, Esser was quoted in the French
daily newspaper *Le Figaro* as saying "Vivendi is our closest partner, we
have the same strategic vision." Other reports also suggested that Vivendi
and Mannesmann planned to create a joint holding company covering
Mannesmann's industrial activities, Vivendi's water and waste treatment
services and both companies' telecoms businesses. Meanwhile Chris Gent
told one reporter that this was an unlikely scenario: "An alliance between
Mannesmann and Vodafone creates much more value than an alliance
between Mannesmann and Vivendi. We can offer a global presence, rather
than just a European one, and a better partnership." Later he told another
that Vivendi would not be able to afford the deal: "Our share exchange
offer [for Mannesmann] is worth . . . much more than Vivendi could offer."

Away from the public rebuttals, dismissals and disclaimers, a very different battle was taking place. The deal between Mannesmann and Vivendi had actually been very close for some time. For nearly a year Esser and Jean-Marie Messier, then Vivendi's high-profile CEO, had discussed a merger of the two groups in detail. A merger document had even been drawn up, under which Mannesmann, with its larger market value, would have held a majority stake. The idea was that the combined group would then sell off Vivendi's water, electricity and rail interests.

The deal came very close indeed, but there always seemed to be a hitch. For example, although Messier and Esser had agreed to be co-chairmen, there were question marks over who would take the top positions elsewhere in the new organization and, according to Esser, also at least four other points, including the key question of the share exchange ratio of the merger. Accounts vary greatly over how serious a disagreement this was or even what happened next, just as each half of a bickering couple seeks to apportion blame following the breakdown of their relationship.

Messier claims that Esser sent a contentious fax to his home in Rambouillet outside Paris on Saturday January 22. Even though the two were having trouble agreeing on which people should fill which positions, the fax apparently questioned a previously agreed parity of numbers on the board of the merged group. Only a few hours later, says Messier, he sent a reply announcing a breakdown in negotiations because "Klaus Esser had breached our pact of trust".

If this really was the formal end of negotiations then Esser didn't seem to understand the fact. Esser suggests that he had been merely looking to secure a seat on the board for Hans Snook of Orange, the company whose acquisition by Mannesmann had so enraged Gent in the first place. It is not clear whether Messier did send the reply to the fax, whether Esser did receive it or whether somehow it was illegible or even misdirected. But what is clear is that, whether through desperation or simply denial, Esser did not behave like a man who had just been dumped.

Esser worked hard to salvage the deal but by now Messier had imposed extra conditions. He demanded that Vivendi executives should hold most of the top positions below Esser and himself. Esser rejected these conditions, which he says would have amounted to a capitulation: "We would have been diluting value for our shareholders in return for the favour of being rescued from a black knight."

Even if Esser genuinely believed that the deal was still on, then it still seems strange that he did not take another hint from Messier. By Monday January 24 Vivendi's entire negotiating team had abruptly checked out of their Düsseldorf hotel and headed home to France. It certainly seemed as though Messier was the one who was looking for an excuse to get out of the deal.

By January 28 a Vivendi board meeting gathered at its headquarters near the Arc de Triomphe to examine the merger deal. Although originally called to approve the merger agreement, the furious faxes had changed everything. The Vivendi board rejected the deal, while at the same time turning its back on rival proposals by BT and the Dutch KPN for a pan-European internet alliance. Although the deal was off between Vivendi and Mannesmann, it seems as though no one, even now, chose to tell Esser. Esser himself is adamant: "By January 29 I certainly did not feel as though the deal had collapsed." Whether Esser knew or not, why had the deal fallen apart so suddenly? And why, when there were so many offers on the table in a frenzied climate of telecoms mergers and acquisitions, did Vivendi choose to reject them all? The simple answer was that there was a better offer waiting in the wings. And the offer came from Chris Gent.

Esser later indicated to the *Financial Times* that he felt betrayed by Messier when he started talking to Vodafone: "When Vodafone launched its bid in October [1999], I knew Chris Gent would approach Vivendi. So I told Messier he was at liberty to talk to other groups, but not to Vodafone, which he agreed was a fair request." However, Messier says he does not recall this request from Esser in one of his recent autobiographies.

Yet Messier and Gent were talking – and making rapid progress. Vodafone came to an arrangement with Vivendi to create a Europe-wide internet service that appeared to undercut one of Mannesmann's main lines of defence against Vodafone, namely the latter's lack of internet capacity. Both sides believed that the joint venture would open the way for market dominance in the field of internet access. Gent agreed to fly over to Paris with his team on Sunday January 30 to seal the deal. He already had another appointment in Paris with Klaus Esser that day so it was no extra trouble, he told Messier.

Knowing that events were conspiring against him, Esser had already arranged to meet Gent and the Vodafone team at the Hyatt hotel near Charles de Gaulle airport in Paris on that day, and it was a meeting he was not looking forward to. His desperation was compounded as he learned from a phone call on the way to the airport that not only was his deal with Vivendi off, but that Vivendi's deal with Vodafone was now a strong possibility.

As he met Gent and his colleagues (comprising Julian Horn-Smith and numerous representatives from Vodafone's team of bankers) at the hotel, the atmosphere was polite but frosty. When Gent arrived, according to the *Sunday Times*, Esser shook his hand and said "thank you for coming over". "That's OK," replied Gent, "we were coming over for a meeting in any case." Vodafone's team later claimed that at this moment the faces of Esser and his team froze as they realized that Vivendi and Vodafone were talking. But in fact Esser already knew of the likelihood of the Vodafone–Vivendi deal and when Gent later added "you are going to lose this thing," Esser knew in his heart that the Englishman was right. The German said nothing though, partly because he hoped that Gent's deal would flounder in the same way that his had and perhaps he was not ready, just yet, to admit defeat. In any case, Gent saw no reason to force humiliation on his rival there and then. News of the Vodafone–Vivendi deal would be out soon enough. It would boost Vodafone's share price further and make a deal with Mannesmann a formality. Both he and Esser knew it.

In winning over Messier in his meeting on the same day, however, Gent had to give some ground. He agreed with Messier that he would discuss the sale to Vivendi of all or part of the German company's fixed line operations in Germany and Italy. He also agreed to sell Vivendi half of Mannesmann's 15% stake in Cegetel, the holding company for fixed and mobile services in France. Because Vivendi already owned 44% of Cegetel, this deal would take Vivendi above the 50% threshold. In the event, Vivendi declined to buy either and Gent's relations with the French giant would ultimately turn sour.

For Esser, things went from bad to worse. Hours after his meeting with Gent, he got the confirmation he had been dreading. He and his downcast advisers from Morgan Stanley and Merrill Lynch heard details of an agreement between Vodafone and Vivendi to form a joint company, Vivazzi, to deliver data and internet services via mobile phones across Europe. As Messier and Gent shook hands on their deal in Paris, the former told the latter that he was sure that Vodafone would win its battle with Mannesmann. And according to the *Sunday Times*, one of the Mannesmann investment bankers remarked bitterly: "Well, what do you expect from Messier? After all, he is not only a former investment banker, he is French."

The Vivendi–Vodafone deal was a crushing blow for Esser and Mannesmann. In public, Esser still declared that he was not interested in sitting down and doing a deal with Vodafone. He pointed out his company's growth potential and what he saw as his superior strategy of integrating land line and mobile telephony. At one investor meeting Esser had told his audience that "the value of Mannesmann is significantly higher than the offer on the table," and claimed that Vodafone's business strategy was changing every few days. He was also dismissive of his old rival's tactics, suggesting that Gent had gone back to his "bad old habits" of negotiating a hostile takeover through the press.

The endgame

This sounded like a final desperate attempt at rhetoric and, behind the scenes, Esser's Mannesmann team knew that all was lost. One of Esser's close aides says: "The failure of the talks with Vivendi, followed by their deal with Vodafone, was the point at which we all realized we had lost the battle. I remember that Sunday really, really clearly. Everybody, including us and most people in the market, thought Mannesmann could get an arrangement with Vivendi. I don't know how close we came to a deal, but I do know that Klaus seemed very, very confident. There were rumours that Vodafone and Vivendi were negotiating, but lots more rumours about ourselves and Vivendi, so we weren't that worried. When the bad news came, it was a big personal blow to Esser – and for the rest of us it was a massive shock." Would a deal with Vivendi have made all the difference for Mannesmann? The aide says: "Well, it's impossible to say for sure. But, yes, it certainly would have helped us a lot."

As January came to an end, the shell-shocked Esser began to think the unthinkable. The deadline for shareholders in early February was approaching rapidly and Vodafone held all the aces. Its deal with Vivendi had undercut one of Mannesmann's main lines of defence, Vodafone's lack of internet capacity. All seemed lost and Esser was not short of comment from others feeling the same way. Most suggested that Mannesmann chief executive Klaus Esser would have little choice now but to sit down and talk about a friendly merger with Gent. "From a shareholders' point of view, if Mannesmann is going to look after its investors, now is the time to sit down with Vodafone and thrash out some recommended deal," said Tressan McCarthy of Credit Lyonnnais Securities. "Many German investors think there is merit in Gent's strategy and that the price is a good one," added Robert Vinall, a telecoms analyst at DG Bank in Frankfurt.

While analysts are important for the information they feed to shareholders, it was the views of the major shareholders themselves that counted most. By continuing to resist the Vodafone bid, Esser risked knocking the Mannesmann price down and incurring their wrath. Even the major shareholders that had backed Mannesmann were rethinking their strategies. Hutchison Whampoa, which owned a 10% stake in Mannesmann, indicated through its bankers that if Gent's team garnered more than 50%, Hutchison would not block the deal. Canning Fok, head of Hutchison Telecom, encouraged Esser to give in, as did Jürgen Schrempp, chairman of DaimlerChrysler and a member of Mannesmann's supervisory board. Schrempp suggested that only two things counted in deciding whether the offer was a good one: whether it was good for the shareholders and whether it made commercial sense. Schrempp told Esser to settle for a minority 49% shareholding and get on with the rest of his life. By now, the battered Esser felt obliged to agree.

Many German fund managers, meanwhile, still feared the hostile nature of the deal and its impact on management problems, though they couldn't help but see its logical financial benefits. And money was talking in another way, of course. Once the bid seemed to be a fait accompli, Mannesmann shareholders started to get excited. The share price rose sharply and even passed the level that Esser had originally said was Mannesmann's true worth. "He has done well to get more out of Gent," said a German shareholder, "but now is the time to stop fighting and start talking."

So that's what Esser and the management team did. Although the public rhetoric continued, advisers of the rival phone companies began "back channel" talks aimed at resolving the battle and opening the way for a friendly merger after all. Gent flew out to Düsseldorf on February 1 from Brize Norton in Vodafone's HS125 jet. Although the Vodafone press office claimed that he had no plans for meeting Esser, it seemed difficult to believe that Gent had gone solely to attend the telecoms conference taking place in the city on that day.

The talks were by now an open secret. Although Mannesmann's official spokesman was still insisting that Esser hadn't met with Gent, by February 2 Mannesmann executives, who by now had all but given up the ghost, were confirming that its top executives had met. Mannesmann supervisory board member, Lars Berg, speaking to institutional investors at the conference said that the two sides had come close to a friendly partnership, although there was still plenty of haggling over numbers. Meanwhile Fabian Kirchmann, another senior executive, told reporters at the same conference that Mannesmann chief executive Klaus Esser and his Vodafone counterpart, Chris Gent, had been in contact numerous times over the previous fortnight.

Now everyone knew that the two sides were talking. The following day,

Thursday February 3, Gent flew again to Düsseldorf with a final offer. The two chief executives had hammered out the basis for a deal during a late-night session the previous evening but there were still some details to be resolved, sufficiently serious to unstitch the deal. First of all there was disagreement over the terms, with some of the more gung-ho Vodafone executives pushing for the immediate resignation of the supervisory board members. Meanwhile, Mannesmann insisted on Vodafone dropping its plan to sell off its fixed-line interests in Germany and Italy.

Esser managed to extract other concessions for Mannesmann. The final agreement was based on an improved share exchange ratio which effectively increased Vodafone's offer by £5.3bn. Furthermore, the agreement defined some terms for the integration of the two companies and their further strategic development. Thereby, it was determined that – for example – Düsseldorf would be retained as one of two dual European headquarters.

Then there was the question of Esser's own compensation, the precise details of which would dog Esser and members of his former board in the courts and (indirectly) bother Gent for months and years to come. To this day, what was agreed on this issue and why is shrouded in mystery. As one Mannesmann aide puts it: "All I know is that there were only a few people present, a few investment bankers, Gent and Esser. And that was all." It was not until a little after 10.30 in the evening local time on Thursday February 3 that a deal was reached in the 21st floor conference room in Mannesmann's high rise building overlooking the Rhine in Düsseldorf.

The following morning Klaus Esser emerged from a meeting of the board to announce that the management of Vodafone AirTouch and Mannesmann had reached an agreement on terms for a recommended merger. At the time the deal was struck in early February, it was worth £115bn

($182bn) and created what at the time was Europe's largest company. It also became the world's fourth largest with a market capitalization of $365bn (£228bn), behind Microsoft ($532bn), General Electric ($445bn) and Cisco Systems ($403bn). Even if it had all been distinctly shotgun, this was the biggest corporate marriage in history. The deal was the world's largest takeover, just ahead of AOL–TimeWarner ($181bn), and well beyond the next contenders, MCIWorldCom–Sprint ($127bn), Pfizer–Warner Lambert ($88bn) and Exxon–Mobil ($86bn). Value on the stock market can be a misleading thing and on different measures there were other companies that were substantially larger at that time. For example, Bayer, the chemical conglomerate, employed five times as many workers worldwide, had three times the turnover and one and a half times the profitability. Yet Bayer (with a market capitalization of $30bn) was not even a tenth of the share value of the newly merged firm. Why? Because the expectation was that the Vodafone's share price would carry on increasing.

In spite of the announcement, Klaus Esser remained defiant. The new non-executive vice-chairman of the merged company insisted that shareholders had been swayed by short-term financial gain. At a news conference, he reminded everyone of the concessions he had won and claimed that 90% of the shareholders believed that Mannesmann would have had better long-term prospects as an independent company. Mannesmann's shares had doubled in value since the bid was launched in November, he also reminded his audience, with a massive impact on the overall value of the deal. Esser's aide recalls: "Klaus was totally defiant that day. Vodafone didn't get us cheap, especially when you look at what has happened to the stock markets since. It wasn't what we wanted, but it was clearly what the Mannesmann shareholders wanted. And in the end, who could really blame them?"

By February 10 the shareholders had made a clear decision. Vodafone announced that it had secured over 60% of Mannesmann's capital. Trading in the new Vodafone shares to be issued in exchange for Mannesmann shares began on that day. The London stock exchange announced special measures to deal with an anticipated avalanche of trade in them. The enlarged company at that time accounted for about 15% of the FTSE 100 index and dealers wanted these special measures to deal with a surge in demand as index tracker funds were permitted to buy the heavyweight stock to reflect its increased weighting in the FTSE 100. Meanwhile, a day earlier, the Deutsche Boerse slipped out a statement saying that it planned to remove Mannesmann from the Xetra Dax 30 index as soon as possible.

Even though the shareholders had decided, there was still plenty of haggling. Even on February 10 the Mannesmann board had still to give the official seal of approval for the deal, although that was in itself a formality now that the agreement was supposed to be "friendly". There were, however, seven hours of talks between the two sides, ostensibly to finalize details. Still, in the context of months of rancorous negotiations, claims and counterclaims in a bidding battle mixing big business, politics and union uproar, seven hours – to the executives of Vodafone and Mannesmann – seemed like the blink of an eye.

Many commentators speculated that the outcome of the takeover battle had left Germany's business culture irreversibly changed. The success of Vodafone was expected to trigger a wave of foreign interest in German companies. The deal was welcomed grudgingly by Gerhard Schröder, who had initially criticized the hostile bid. Tony Blair was predictably more enthusiastic and looked forward to a level playing field for British companies in Europe. Others were less sure. Ulrich Schröder, an economist with Deutsche Bank in Frankfurt at the time, said that he doubted whether there would be a rush to acquire other German companies in the wake of the Mannesmann deal. "There are very few companies with that kind of wide ownership on the stock market that can be bought in Germany," he said. So far, his view seems to have been borne out.

Many were disturbed at the high cost paid by both Vodafone and Mannesmann in fighting each other. One estimate suggested that Mannesmann and Vodafone together spent some $1bn on advertising and consultation fees during the takeover battle. The World Socialist website observed, with characteristic bitterness, "This sum corresponds to what 280,000 people on social security in Berlin would receive in six months . . . this enormous expenditure on advertising appears nonsensical, since it is the large investors – the investment funds, financial houses and pension fund managers – who decided on the takeover. They make their decisions based on economic data, not advertising slogans, pictures of yuppies, babies and naked bosoms, such as appeared day after day in full-page ads in all German newspapers."

It was an extreme view and it didn't stop the wheels of capitalism rolling along. As expected Vodafone had to spin off Orange to satisfy regulatory concerns, although the European Commission didn't officially confirm this until April, long after a similar ruling by the UK authorities. France Telecom were also known to be interested and eventually bought Orange for the inflated price of £31bn. Viking Kjellstrom, telecoms analyst with HSBC, believes that this was the beginning of the end for technology stocks: "It was when France Telecom decided to buy Orange in the UK that the bubble really burst."

Esser, meanwhile, temporarily found a place on the Vodafone board, but it was to prove a brief encounter. The announcement of his formal, mutually agreed departure came in the autumn of 2000. A few days after the takeover deal in February 2000, however, it became public that Esser would give up his executive responsibilities. The European Industrial Relations Observatory put the figure for his payment at nearly DM60m (over €30m). This, they said, was made up of three major components. Firstly a continuation of Klaus Esser's basic payment and annual bonuses until June 30, 2004, the date when his employment contract was due to run out (worth DM15.2m). Secondly, a special bonus of "nine annual salaries" (worth DM12.6m). Finally a so-called "appreciation award" of DM31.1m paid by Vodafone.

It was the last of these payments that caused lingering problems for Vodafone and major problems for Esser himself. By April 2001, Esser was having to deny accusations that he had given up the ghost of the Vodafone defence in exchange for the promise of an inflated redundancy payment. A month earlier, he had been put under investigation by the Düsseldorf prosecutor for the alleged payments. The prosecutor's investigation centred on the week beginning January 22, 2000, when Esser and Messier gave contradictory accounts over the state of play between Mannesmann and Vivendi over their proposed merger. Those seeking a prosecution alleged that Esser's mind may have been clouded by the severance payment, which was twice the sum that Mannesmann was contractually obliged to pay him. Esser's defenders, however, pointed out that the exceptionally large payment was partly due to the fact that, almost uniquely in the telecommunications industry (although not for a German chief executive), Esser had no stock options. After a lengthy investigation German prosecutors charged six former directors of Mannesmann in February 2003, alleging illegal payments made during the Vodafone takeover. Although the six were not named, Esser has admitted to being on the list and the case is pending. Gent had been formally cleared of any wrongdoing by the Düsseldorf State Prosecutor's office earlier in the investigation.

To rub salt into Esser's wounds, Messier had written a book in 2000 in which he suggested that Esser knew that their deal would not be on by mid-January. Esser denied the accusation and counterclaimed that his improved severance package was set up by Mannesmann's compensation committee on February 4, the day after he had conceded defeat. The two have since been involved in a ugly legal spat over who said what to whom, and when. Messier has also since left the Vivendi board.

While Esser and Messier had become embroiled in recriminations, Gent had emerged, bruised but triumphant, from a battle that many had doubted he could win three months earlier. But when he recalled his triumph in an interview with the *Financial Times* his highlight was something altogether more personal. On the night of the deal, he chose to fly home in Vodafone's corporate jet and land at Brize Norton airport shortly before dawn. "That morning was the first occasion I had seen my son, who was 10 months old at the time, in a little while, and he threw his plates and tray on the floor in excitement when I came in through the door. 'Here he is, as seen on TV,' said my wife."

It had certainly been an astonishing and punishing year of deal making from AirTouch to Verizon Wireless, to the biggest of them all in Mannesmann. But for now Chris Gent felt like he was at the top of a rollercoaster, looking down on the rest of the world.

PART 2

Life on Top of the Rollercoaster

Red Devils and Prancing Horses

The year had been an exhilarating one for Chris Gent, and for Vodafone. In January 1999 Vodafone had been a British mobile phone operator with a handful of overseas businesses. By early 2000 the company had undertaken three massive deals which had catapulted them into a massive global operator. Now with technology stocks reaching new heights, Gent and Vodafone had become massive success stories, the darlings of the media and investors.

The same could not be said for Vodafone's newly acquired customers, many of whom seemed unfamiliar with the Vodafone brand. Although Gent had successfully built the company in a year of frenzied acquisition, it was not clear to many in the world what Vodafone stood for. Many of the businesses that Vodafone had acquired had no trace of the Vodafone name, while the group's sponsorship efforts, via the England cricket team and local horse racing, hardly had international reach. The next obvious task was to generate a global brand to make the most of the company's global power. Gent and his team chose to do this through the sexiest high-profile sponsorship deals possible: with Manchester United, the biggest football club in the world and with Ferrari, the top motor racing team.

Why had Vodafone's external image lagged behind the development of the actual business? Given the breathtaking pace of change in the business it would be hard for any branding campaign to keep pace, but was especially so when the business drivers' minds were focused on the bottom line. As one branding consultant closely linked to Vodafone explains: "Vodafone, from Harrison to Whent and through to Gent, were a bunch of entrepreneurs who drove the business bloody hard and basically got what they went out to get. Everything was, and to this day still is, driven by a desire to hit the bottom-line targets. These guys were brilliant at making things happen but, in keeping with many entrepreneurs, saw things like sponsorship as a sort of 'let-your-hair-down' thank you to suppliers and staff. It got the Vodafone name out there and that was important to them, but they didn't have a sophisticated understanding of what building a brand really meant."

Part of the reason was that they had never really needed to. Back in the 1980s and early 1990s Vodafone had not been able to sell direct to the end-user. Although in at the birth of the wireless market in the early 1980s, Vodafone, along with its rival Cellnet (as it was then called), was forced by the rules of its cellular licence to operate through intermediaries or "service providers". They could not sell airtime direct to consumers. The whole market changed in 1993 when Orange and One2One launched. Not only were the new boys allowed from the start to sell their services direct to the consumer, but they seemed more adept at branding than Vodafone. Orange, in particular, was very good at the 'feelgood' factor about its product; Vodafone was not.

By the late 1990s Vodafone's old ways of promoting itself began to look rather amateurish. It still ran its sponsorship largely through the corporate affairs department. When Vodafone thought about branding at all, it thought about the sponsorship of sporting events. Gerry Whent, Gent's predecessor, offered generous hospitality on racecourses and golf courses throughout the UK; Whent and his chairman Ernie Harrison were sports mad. Harrison shared Whent's passion for horse racing, which eventually resulted in Vodafone's sponsorship of the Derby. Then new chairman Iain MacLaurin's chairmanship of the England and Wales Cricket Board, combined with Gent's own well-known enthusiasm for the game were undoubtedly factors in securing Vodafone's sponsorship of the England cricket team, a deal that runs until 2005.

Viking Kjellstrom, telecoms analyst at HSBC, suggests that the wrong kind of sponsorship actually created a very negative image for the company among European investors: "I think that there are differing attitudes to sponsorship depending on where you are. The Anglo-Saxon investors in the UK are always favourable to a lot of horse racing and cricket and so on. But there are doubts among European investors, employees and customers. People would look and say 'Chris Gent is more interested in horse racing and cricket than actually running the business'." And when you've just successfully bought Mannesmann in the biggest hostile takeover in corporate history and you're trying to build a decent working relationship with your new employees, this sort of thing doesn't go down to well with them. "They got the impression that all these Vodafone executives do is go around to all the sporting events and drink cocktails. It makes one fear more for the livers of Gent and his team," Kjellstrom added.

The branding consultant says: "Everyone may have had a jolly good time in the corporate boxes but in terms of building the company brand worldwide, sponsoring the Derby and the England Cricket team was a glorious example of money badly spent. When your old CEO is an avowed horse racing fan who likes nothing better than a good day on the Downs, it's no wonder you sponsor the Vodafone Derby. And when your Chairman is also in charge of the EWCB, it's no surprise when your name ends up on the England cricket shirt, even if England haven't won the Ashes almost for as long as Vodafone has been around as a company. Everyone at

Vodafone may wax lyrical about how wonderful it has been to be associated with this or that, but once you suddenly have a global powerhouse on your hands, as Vodafone did, you need to be a bit cleverer and think of the business reasons why you're supporting something through sponsorship."

Global branding

So it was that as Gent flew back from Düsseldorf with a global reputation as a deal maker, he needed to move in order to ensure that the company developed a global brand in keeping with Vodafone's new found status. Why was it so important to get a global brand? Because selling one brand across the world is far more powerful and cost effective than selling lots of different brands in different countries. Ordinary people in Germany and Italy were more likely to have heard of D2 and Omnitel than Vodafone, yet the latter now owned the former two, plus several other brands in many other countries. Central to the concerns of Paul Donovan, Vodafone UK's commercial and marketing director (now CEO of Vodafone Ireland), was the knowledge that in spite of its size, Vodafone at the time of the deal with Manchester United was spending less on advertising than its competitors, lagging a poor fourth with an advertising spend of £31m a year, well behind One2One, BT Cellnet and Orange, as they were then known.

Manchester United

Gent still wanted to maintain the group's reputation for the sponsorship of sport. Sports sponsorship of the right kind was undoubtedly worthwhile, with great potential to more than recoup outlay through global exposure via television to the youthful audience most likely to buy Vodafone's products. Furthermore, brands were becoming more and more important to mobile operators and when sponsoring Gent wanted Vodafone to be aligned not only to a winning team, but also to bigger and better brands which would be recognized right across the world. The Vodafone team had been trying to tie up a sponsorship deal with the biggest football club in the world for some time. Now, as the Mannesmann deal fell into place, so did another. It was announced that Vodafone had signed a four year sponsorship deal with perhaps the best known football club in the world, Manchester United. At the time of the deal they were the reigning FA Premier League Champions, FA Cup holders and, most impressively of all, had triumphed in the European Champions League following their dramatic last gasp 2–1 win over Bayern Munich in Barcelona's magnificent Nou Camp stadium in May 1999. By comparison with Vodafone, at this point the UK's largest company, Manchester United was tiny – but its brand exposure across the world in the world's most popular game gave Vodafone a platform that it could not get elsewhere.

Under the terms of the agreement, Vodafone was to pay Manchester United £30m over four years for the privilege of sponsorship. Donovan claimed that the sponsorship deal would enable the two brands to enter new markets. He said: "Vodafone and Manchester United are both ambitious champions that are used to being – and staying – number one." Predictable rhetoric but, certainly at the time, the deal was generally praised as a marriage of giants. Writing in the (now sadly defunct) *Industry Standard*, Matthew Yeomans claimed that the new deal "with what is now the largest telecommunications company in the world looks set to change the face of modern sport." And according to Michael Peters, founder of the communications and branding consultancy, The Identica Partnership, the logic of aligning two strong brands is obvious: "Put simply, strong brands sell. The power of brands is undeniable and aligning two strong brands with each other can provide even greater reach and effectiveness."

Donovan certainly knew a thing or two about powerful brands. He had worked with many of the biggest in his time. Starting off at Mars, he had moved to Coca-Cola and then had become marketing director of Apple Computer. His move into telecoms came with a job as head of business marketing at BT. This was followed by a move to One2One as commercial director and a spell at Cable & Wireless Optus before arriving at Vodafone. He had been credited by the advertising industry bible, *Campaign*, with building the One2One brand and he hoped that he could repeat that success with the more established Vodafone name. Donovan's shortfall on this particular deal was a personal rather than professional one. He was (and is) an Arsenal fan.

The deal transformed Vodafone's global image. As everyone knows, Manchester United is no ordinary club. With over a £1 billion in turnover each year only the likes of Real Madrid (sponsored by Siemens IC mobile) and Bayern Munich (sponsored by Deutsche Telekom) rival it in sheer size. More importantly for Vodafone, the exposure that Manchester United commands is global. Manchester United players are treated like gods in the Far East, where the fan base is huge with, for example, more Chinese Manchester United fans than there are English ones. And Vodafone had business interests in China, Japan and other Asian countries who could be reached through an association with the Manchester United brand.

There was another reason why Vodafone was so excited about the deal. This was to be a commercial alliance and not just a mere sponsorship. The deal extended beyond shirts and hospitality into the digital realm. Fans would be able to buy branded mobile phones and access the internet. The idea from the outset was that fans would be able to see highlights of Manchester United matches and watch classic goals on their mobile phones whenever and wherever they chose. Vodafone also designed a United Pay as You Talk mobile phone that it planned to sell to fans selected through direct mail from the club's supporter database, which included details of Old Trafford season-ticket holders as well as club members. And it kicked off a series of direct marketing projects to promote its new manUmobile WAP portal and text messaging service. The manUmobile service was based on the official Manchester United web site and offered goal alerts, match reports and team news and was designed to build in audio interviews, video clips and merchandise offers.

From the Manchester United point of view, telecoms was the sector with which to be linked. They had been associated with the same sponsor, Sharp, for about eighteen years but they now found themselves linked to a global powerhouse whose leader seemed to be chalking up one success after another. Vodafone was certainly number one in its field and like Manchester United, had achieved a great treble with its three deals for AirTouch, Verizon Wireless and Mannesmann. And it seemed that mobile phones would soon become the de facto internet access device. From a business point of view it seemed hard to fault the deal.

To be fair, much of the football world was getting excited about the internet at the time and Europe's football authorities were anxious to get in on the money making. In the same week as the Vodafone–Manchester United commercial deal, UEFA, European soccer's governing body, claimed that internet broadcast rights, gaming and other commercial investments could provide around €1bn for Europe's top teams over the next 10 years – with the bulk going to monster clubs like United.

As we now know, the heady commercial expectations of the internet were not realized. But at the time the only people with misgivings seemed to be fans of the game. The Manchester United fanzine *The Devil May Care* was predictably disgusted on hearing of the deal: "[There's] only one winner and ultimately that is Vodafone – not Manchester United . . . the name of another company emblazoned on the red shirt is an insult to our great club. Wouldn't it have been superb if we'd stuck up two fingers to a shirt sponsorship deal and gone it alone like the maverick club we are supposed to be? . . . Still, I suppose we should be grateful they didn't sell their souls to Orange – the mind boggles."

Although the internet has been a disappointment, in many senses the deal has worked very well indeed for Vodafone. Nigel Currie, director of Gem Europe and chairman of the European Sponsorship Consultants Association, whose company was responsible for helping the deal to become a success for both sides, says "Given the eighteen years with Sharp, the association of fans with Vodafone in truth all happened a lot quicker than we had expected. In a short period of time the exposure levels were high and the brand recognition was strong. Selling new shirts helped as the fans wanted to keep up with the look."

Other things like the demand for latest pictures of Beckham playing in his ever-changing haircut meant that the Vodafone brand went out all over the world. The impact of Beckham is perhaps a unique issue for both Manchester United and Vodafone. His ability as a footballer, combined with good looks and a glamorous lifestyle, have already had sponsors like Adidas, Police sunglasses and Brylcreem showering millions of pounds upon him as an individual. His pulling power is so obvious that Vodafone were desperate to feature him in their ad campaigns. But a prolonged period of wrangling between Beckham and his club over his personal image rights prevented them from using him until recently. When Beckham did sort out a new contract with Manchester United, £20,000 of his £90,000-a-week contract was from image rights alone.

The Vodafone deal with Manchester United must be judged a success. Research showed that by mid-2001 Vodafone already had the highest recall of any Premier League shirt sponsor. PR firm Propeller Direction scoured national newspapers in April and May to establish how much picture coverage major brands received in the news sections alone. Top of the pile came Vodafone, although Propeller's marketing director Marilyn Wicks attributed some of the success to the extensive coverage gained from the serial prankster Karl Power's appearance in the Manchester United team photo just before a vital European Champions League match.

Whether the business returns though products and services via Manchester United fans have been such a success is less clear. The devil is locked in the detail of the deal, says Oliver Butler, editor of *Soccer Investor*: "In these deals, Vodafone don't just hand over £30 million like that and go away for four years. Some of the money is guaranteed as a basic payment, but then there is a performance related element for all the business spin-offs. When the media quote the £30 million, they don't know how much belongs to each category. So it's difficult to know whether Vodafone feels it has value for money or not from the deal."

Given that Vodafone set out to become a global brand, this side of the project has to be judged a success as well. And as the benefits of the United deal became clear, Gent ordered a fresh look at the way in which the emerging Vodafone global brand could be exploited. By October 2000, Vodafone was asking major ad agencies to pitch for a pan-European account that would be worth as much as £50m, much of which would be aimed at exploiting the link with a big name like Manchester United. While the sums were large, the Vodafone account represented a puzzle to many ad agencies. Although the brand's logo – the red quotation marks – had a big presence in the high street, the terms of its original mobile licence (forbidding it from selling its brand directly) meant that the Vodafone name itself conveyed surprisingly little to consumers.

Rebranding

The Manchester United sponsorship and the review of its advertising strategy were good starts, but more was needed. Vodafone had to look around for new talent and in November 2000, the company hired Coca-Cola executive David Haines as its first global brand director. With different brands all over Europe, never mind the world, Gent realized he needed to rebrand the European subsidiary companies over which it had control.

Haines had a great track record. He had previously held senior posts at Mars and Unilever. At the former he had held various sales, marketing and management positions before becoming its European marketing director. At the latter, he was based both in Hamburg and London. Once he arrived at Vodafone he was to report to Thomas Geitner, the Vodafone director nominally responsible for global branding and someone from Mannesmann who, as Gent had promised, would prosper in the new enlarged Vodafone regime. Haines was clear about what he was trying to achieve. "We are building real value. This is about business, not marketing nor the glitzy world of advertising on its own. This is about building value for our shareholders and in the end getting a brand that is worth a lot of money."

Haines didn't really waste much time in ringing the changes. Vodafone had employed the ad agency BMP DDB since 1996 but it was unceremoniously dropped. A series of changes then took place which has resulted in the current structure, in which Wieden & Kennedy are Vodafone's global advertising agency, J. Walter Thompson (JWT) being used in its subsidiary company countries and with WCRS, the agency that built the Orange brand, handing over to JWT in the UK.

The brief for those left with Vodafone's business was not exactly modest.

Haines wanted to create the first truly global mobile service brand and by mid 2001 they had shown their intentions by appointing two more heavy-weights to the Vodafone team. They brought former One2One marketer Colin Morley in as brand and channel marketing director, and former Motorola marketer Rob Schweidler as head of corporate marketing. Donovan, who had himself been at One2One, admitted the ground that Vodafone had to make up. He told *Marketing*: "We've recognized the importance of brand advertising in driving business objectives. It's fair to say Orange has demonstrated more consistency (in its ads) than Voda-fone, One2One and BT Cellnet."

Chris Gent's desire to create a global brand, alongside the Manchester United deal and appointment of Haines and other heavyweights, had made a good start. Gent, though not a big football fan himself, had readily understood the commercial appeal of Manchester United. But Vodafone had lot of image problems still in Europe, where the Mannesmann battle had been fought and won and this was where there were significant gaps in the sponsorship portfolio.

Ferrari

When Gent and his team looked around for images of global supremacy they had a number of options. One of the official sponsorship berths for the Olympics or World Cup would have been a possibility, but both only came along once every four years and Gent wanted something with more regular exposure. But with Europe in mind, Vodafone headed in a differ-ent direction. They kept coming back to the same image time after time after time: World Formula One motor racing champion, the German Michael Schumacher, winning yet another race in his Italian Ferrari, the most famous racing car in the world.

The history of Ferrari is in itself a fascinating story. Ferrari's founder, racing legend Enzo Ferrari, engineered his sports cars with a single object-ive in mind: speed. His legacy became appealing only to professional racers or daredevils. When the great man died in 1988, however, the com-pany was nearly bankrupt. Difficult years followed until Ferrari's owners, Fiat, in the shape of its then chairman, the late Gianni Agnelli, hand-picked Luca di Montezemolo to revive it.

Agnelli and di Montezemolo's father were old and close friends. Yet Montezemolo Jr had already worked for both car makers earlier in his career before making a name for himself in marketing at Cinzano, the liquor company. But his major triumph before his move to Ferrari had been his role organizing Italy's 1990 World Cup. The football tournament, through its mix of great football and a dramatic operatic backdrop from the likes of Luciano Pavarotti, was a huge financial and PR success.

Montezemolo had been in charge of Ferrari since 1992. Elegantly dressed, charming and with a broad smile, it is no surprise to find that an Italian women's magazine ranked him as one of its top ten examples of "ideal masculine beauty" – just behind Sean Connery and Harrison Ford – in a poll of 1,000 Italian women. Montezemolo was indignant, complaining to the magazine's editors about the poll, saying "I am a manager, not a movie star." But what a manager. Back in 1992, Ferrari was going nowhere. Losing millions of dollars a year, Montezemolo risked $80m more to modernize the factories. He brought in engineers and designers from Fiat to rethink every step of production and design. "Montezemolo is atypical in Italy in business because he follows through," says Francesco Casolari, director of the Industrial Association of Modena. "In Italy, a lot of people do a lot of talk, but little action. He is a man of action." Eight years later, Ferrari was a thriving business once again and, with Schumacher on board, had returned to a position of total supremacy in Formula One racing. It was the global number one and Chris Gent badly wanted a piece of the action.

The price wasn't cheap. When he finally got his way after months of pro-longed negotiation with Ferrari, Gent flew to Monaco in a state of great excitement, and no wonder. The announcement was made on the after-noon of May 25, 2001 in the plush surroundings of the Hotel de Paris and was attended not only by Gent and Montezemolo, but also by Ferrari Sporting Director Jean Todt, World Champion Michael Schumacher and his team mate Rubens Barichello. With Gent himself a major player as chief executive of a global powerhouse, it was unusual to see him appear almost star struck by the attentions of the men from Ferrari. One almost comical photo shows a manically grinning Gent clasping the hand of the sharp-suited Montezemolo for the obligatory handshake pose.

Gent revealed to the press why he seemed so deliriously happy: "We love backing winners. We are the world's leading mobile telecoms company and it is our objective for Vodafone to be recognized as one of the leading global brands. The sponsorship of Ferrari, with the immensely valuable media coverage that Formula One attracts, will help us towards achieving this ambition." The suave Montezemolo put the attraction of the famous Prancing Horse to Gent more in the manner you would expect from an Italian man: "A Ferrari is like a beautiful woman that makes you fall in love at first sight," he said smoothly, albeit sounding alarmingly like Swiss Tony from BBC's *The Fast Show*.

Gent was certainly smitten. In many senses, the partnership between the two red-liveried giants seemed ideal. But, as Montezemolo could have told him, cars – like beautiful women – were pleasing to the eye but heavy on the wallet. The three-year sponsorship deal with the Ferrari Formula One team certainly gave the Vodafone group a more complete global pro-file, but at a price. Financial terms were not disclosed but there was speculation of a possible £35m a year. The idea of the deal was for "signifi-cant" branding for Vodafone to appear on the sides, the noses and the front wings of the cars, as well as on the drivers' overalls and helmets, from the start of the 2002 season. As with the Manchester United deal, it allowed Vodafone to offer Ferrari branded services for the team.

For Ferrari the business rationale was very good. "This is a very important agreement for us as it links us with an international partner, which is very strong in countries that are of great importance for Ferrari, such as Great Britain," said Montezemolo. And no one seemed more delighted than Bernie Ecclestone, effectively the controller of the whole Formula One empire, who saw technology and telecoms as the replacement for the exodus of tobacco advertising from the sport. Certainly, the deal continued what was starting to become a trend. At the time, Arrows were in the second year of a two-year deal with Orange, while computer company Compaq had become a major source of revenue for the Williams team, and McClaren had won sponsorship from Siemens, who manufacture mobile phones.

The deal also covered Ferrari.net, the company that oversees all internet activity for the Ferrari-Maserati group. In addition Montezemolo wanted the fan base of Ferrari to get the latest news from their text messages or pictures of the cars going over the line, the sort of thing that would make lots of money for Vodafone products and services. "It will not only concern all our needs in terms of mobile communication, but also a collaboration on new technologies and the internet," he said. Furthermore, he added: "it means we have reached one of the targets I had set myself, namely to have three major sponsors, as Vodafone lines up alongside Philip Morris and Shell."

Gent's willingness to spend £35m a year, just to be alongside two other sponsors on the blur of a fast moving car, was seen by many as the mark of a company with lots of money to burn. Critics at the time (and there were plenty) pointed to the sponsorship of the Arrows team by Orange at a fraction of the cost of the Vodafone-Ferrari deal. The branding consultant close to Vodafone scoffs at this one: "That's rubbish. Orange wanted their logo all over the Arrows, but the car was never on television because it was at the back of the race. The Orange boys were in bed with a loser. At least every picture in the Vodafone dossier shows a winning team."

A European strategy

Although the deal seemed over-expensive, there was at least a clear logic to it. Vodafone had used the Manchester United sponsorship to build its brand name in Britain and in Manchester United's major markets in the Far East. The Ferrari deal was of course relevant to the global nature of Formula One racing but also fitted very neatly indeed into Vodafone's European strategy. Many of the races in the Formula One season are held in Europe and it was here that the Vodafone brand needed to be built most. The Vodafone consultant says: "When they did the Ferrari deal they were a company with a brand called Vodafone and a whole bunch of other companies in Europe with a brand name of something else. In Germany, Vodafone meant Mannesmann; in Italy, it was Omnitel; in France, SFR; in Spain, Airtel and so on through many other European countries. Even its own UK identity has been confused by changing its name from Vodafone to Vodafone AirTouch and back again. And therefore there's no global brand awareness of the name Vodafone, let alone who they were or what they did."

The consultant continues: "There was much hard work to be done to win people over to the brand name, without losing the goodwill towards the other brand names built up over the years." And the task of building up a brand was not helped by the fact that the European mobile phone market was at different stages of development in different countries. In Finland, for example, people used mobile phones more than they did land lines.

But in Germany only around a third of the 83 million population were using mobiles at the time of the Vodafone deal.

Although Vodafone was trying to appeal to customers across Europe through a single brand, another target of course was the 60,000 people who now found themselves working for Vodafone as the result of its hostile takeover of Mannesmann and its associated businesses, people who maybe didn't really want to be working for the company at all. Not long after Vodafone won the battle with Mannesmann, Gent decided to move quickly on the issue of rebranding. He scrapped the Mannesmann D2 brand name and redubbed it D2 Vodafone. He replaced the familiar blue logo on Mannesmann's high rise in Düsseldorf with the British company's red logo. It Italy, meanwhile, he ditched Vodafone's new subsidiary Omnitel's green logo in favour of a green-and-red Omnitel Vodafone logo. By November 2002, Julian Horn-Smith, the group's chief operating officer, was able to announce: "The Vodafone brand is now present in all our controlled mobile operations, with Japan and Italy expected to move to the single brand in 2003. The association between the brand and the service offerings will intensify and the investment will continue to differentiate us from other customers."

These were politically awkward decisions, but the Ferrari deal was an attempt to redress the balance. Says the Vodafone consultant: "By strange coincidence the two key countries that were carrying different names – D2 and Omnitel – and who put up the most resistance to changing to the Vodafone brand were those who had most to gain from Vodafone's Formula One foray: the Italians because of an association with the Ferrari car and the Germans because of an association with Schumacher. This has meant a hell of a lot to the German and Italian parts of Vodafone's business, although you can hardly tell a hostile workforce that you're doing it to make them less hostile. I think this has to be one of the smartest pieces of sponsorship ever, not only for external customers but also for internal ones as well."

Another source close to Vodafone says: "I honestly believe that this is money well spent. All money needs to get spent strategically. You need to know what you want to do with the money. Yes, sponsoring Ferrari is an expensive business, especially when you add in all sorts of extra marketing costs. But in the end it is cost effective because the same Vodafone advertising has been used in all Vodafone's markets, something which saves lots of money and gives a powerful message. Think about the purchase of Mannesmann which cost over £100 billion, spending £35 million a year of sponsorship money on Ferrari and getting happier German and Italian customers has got to be money well spent."

How are you?

With the Manchester United and Ferrari deals going well, Vodafone rolled out the next phase of its attempts to give itself a global brand image. In September 2001 it launched a new 60-second commercial, part of a £250m global campaign, the largest in its history. The ad, from Wieden & Kennedy, showed a series of cameos held together with a soundtrack by the Dandy Warhols. Caroline Marshall, editor of *Campaign*, explains: "All the cameos are based on the opening of conversations in response to the question 'How are you?' Young people doing music festival type stuff ('we're groovy'), a man at the zoo with his kid ('I'm in a meeting'), three girls in a cab on a night out ('we're gorgeous'), a sea rescue ('we're safe'), a Manchester United football match ('we're winning') – and so on". Although Marshall was not overly impressed by the ad, she admits this effort was a step forward. A year earlier, she notes "Vodafone produced twelve different ads for twelve different markets. It didn't so much have an image problem – the problem was that it didn't even have an image to have a problem with . . ." She goes on: "This is without question the best ad in the history of Vodafone. But after 'Nobody goes further to keep you in touch', X-files parodies and [the slogan] 'You are here', that's not saying very much."

Vodafone spent plenty of money, when at the top of the corporate rollercoaster, associating its name with the likes of Manchester United, Ferrari and an orderly series of consistent global ad messages with a catchy theme tune. One marketing and advertising rule of thumb is that whatever you spend in sponsorship, you need to spend again in promoting that sponsorship, and many commentators claim that Gent and his colleagues at Vodafone threw away money on advertising and continued to waste hundreds of millions of pounds, even when the group's fortunes subsequently declined. Yet had the money not been spent the group would remain an powerful but anonymous holding name for a disparate bunch of rag, tag and bobtail interests dotted around the world. At least the brand was now punching somewhere a little closer to its weight.

6 Trouble in Vodaville

As a triumphant Chris Gent and his team strived successfully to match their global triumphs with a global image for Vodafone, the reputation of the company on its own doorstep began to take a heavy battering.

The headquarters of its global operations are to be found in Newbury. A market town in Berkshire, Newbury is found about five miles south of the M4, the motorway linking London with the west of England. Newbury residents on the whole were delighted to have such a major employer in their midst, but for some there was a feeling of discomfort as Vodafone progressed from business offshoot of Racal to global powerhouse. At the centre of concerns was a fear that Vodafone's power had grown so much that the fates of the town and the group had become inextricably linked, so much so that Newbury came to be dubbed by many local residents "Vodaville".

These concerns were based around Vodafone's attempts to flex its considerable corporate muscle on two major – and related – issues. The first was the Newbury bypass, the infamous environmental battleground of the mid-1990s between an ailing Conservative government hell-bent on a transport policy prioritizing road construction above public transport and a zealously hostile and publicity-savvy environmental lobby, personified in the media by Swampy, the self-styled eco-warrior. The second was an attempt by Vodafone to move its staff away form its many locations in the centre of Newbury and into a single, large global headquarters just outside the town. The switch to a central headquarters, on the face of it, made perfect sense for a global economic giant. The problem was that the proposed development was to be found in the middle of rural land protected from development by English environmental laws. Furthermore, it was situated conveniently close to the bypass for which it had so vociferously lobbied.

Ultimately, Vodafone achieved its aims on both the bypass and its headquarters, but in the process managed to display an aggressive, some argued bullying, streak which it exercised upon local and national politicians and local pressure groups. In the words of one local Liberal Democrat councillor: "To be blunt, Vodafone behaved like perfect pigs over the whole business." It also revealed an occasional tendency by Gent, perhaps on the back of his astonishing run of success elsewhere, to take unnecessary chances with the company's fortunes. Vodafone's dealings with Newbury gave it plenty of bad press and brought it embarrassingly close to being forced to undertake a massively costly relocation away from the town. And in the process it brought home to many living in the area a somewhat unhealthy relationship between corporation and community.

At the zenith of Vodafone's powers in the Spring of 2000, a stroll down Newbury's main high street was a pleasant enough experience: a picturesque setting with the famous Newbury racecourse not far away. There are all the usual high street favourites: Boots, The Woolwich and Thomas Cook. But if you looked a little closer at many buildings you would see another corporate name around the town, one with dozens of branches.

If you wandered along and looked at the branding on one building you would see "Vodafone". A couple of doors down there it would be again –

and again, and again. This was no ordinary place. According to a map on Vodafone's own website at the time there were not far short of 50 separate offices in the town. The headquarters of the giant were to be found wrapped around the back of the Curry Garden, Newbury's Tandoori restaurant. The 10% discount on takeaways was a boon for Gent and his colleagues during the long evenings spent discussing the takeovers of AirTouch and Mannesmann.

The higgledy-piggledy intertwining of Vodafone through the fabric of the town was no accident. Sir Gerald Whent, who set up Vodafone's fore-runner, the Racal Telecom Division in the mid-1980s, based his unit in the same town. The company at that time had fewer than 50 employees, all based in one building. When Whent's mini-empire evolved out of Racal into Vodafone, it simply started to buy up more small buildings in the town rather choose a bigger building in a larger town. This reflected the earlier development of Racal itself, pioneered by Sir Ernest Harrison. Both Harrison and Whent believed passionately in the entrepreneurial culture of the small cohesive unit. So Racal had become a number of separate units, each with a close-knit atmosphere and energy. One Racal old-timer recalls: "It's Vodafone this and that now all over Newbury but you used to have Racal, Racal Telecom, Racal this and Racal that all over the place. That was just the culture: it was the way Ernie and Gerry wanted it."

And Whent wanted to be close to the action in Newbury. As Vodafone started to accumulate more and more property within the town, it was suggested by some senior directors at Racal that he would be better off relocating his office back to their headquarters in Bracknell. He refused point blank, saying he would never move away from the business hub. The Vodafone old-timer goes on: "Gerry was always against any kind of consolidation at all. He was quite happy with Vodafone being spread all over the place. Whenever any of the others suggested bringing the various parts of Vodafone together he always completely kicked the idea out of touch."

The idea may have made good business sense to Whent and Harrison but as Vodafone's success grew so did the traffic levels in the town. Just getting through Newbury was slowly becoming a nightmare both for residents and those passing through the town. Adrian Foster-Fletcher, a local businessman and the Newbury coordinator for Friends of the Earth, takes up the story: "They didn't seem to acknowledge it but Vodafone were the cause of the town's gridlock in the first place."

Foster-Fletcher claims that Vodafone themselves discovered that that they were making 1200 journeys a day between their various offices in Newbury, without even starting to count those journeys made at the start of the day coming into Newbury or those at the end of the day as people left. Foster-Fletcher says: "They created two very big bubbles during the day. They had all of their staff arriving at 8.30 a.m. and all of them leaving at 5.30 p.m." Vodafone refused to invest in video technology between offices on the grounds of expense and they wouldn't introduce flexi-time working or hot-desking or any working from home. "At that time, Vodafone really was all very much an old-fashioned 'Reggie Perrin and his boss CJ at Sunshine Desserts' sort of mentality. This was the root of the congestion problem," adds Foster-Fletcher. But instead of adjusting its own practices, Vodafone sought to solve the problem by discouraging the flow of other traffic through the town. The company received flak from local residents and therefore became an enthusiastic supporter of the Newbury bypass.

The Newbury bypass

The A34 Newbury bypass was Britain's most controversial road-building project and saw the country's biggest anti-road protest. Local campaigners formed the Society for the Prevention of a Western Bypass (SPEWBY) and battled long and hard against the road throughout the 1980s. Their efforts led to a public inquiry in 1988. The Thames Valley Police also had doubts about the scheme, predicting in the early 1990s that the bypass would cause a huge rise in the number of road accidents (which proved to be a justified fear when it finally opened).

When the public inquiry found in favour of the road in the mid-1990s, a spectacular protest campaign followed. This incorporated every conceivable form of protest from mass letter writing and lobbying of European institutions to non-violent direct action and criminal damage. Protesters set up camps along the bypass route and opened an office in the town centre in the summer of 1994. Within a few months their concerted campaign had persuaded Transport Secretary Brian Mawhinney to put the road on hold subject to a review. Barely six months later, however, he made an abrupt about turn and gave the bypass the go-ahead, which set the scene for a massive battle of mental and physical wits between security guards and contractors from construction companies on the one side and environmental protesters on the other. The latter stages of the campaign to stop the bypass led to a memorable "direct action" protest that saw around 1000 people arrested. This final phase of the campaign lasted for three months from January to April 1996 and this is the one that most people associate with the fight against the road.

One senior Liberal Democrat who supported the bypass along with Vodafone is glad that he did. He says: "I supported it only marginally, but I fought for the environment and for people in the town, whose lives were going to be much improved. There is much less pollution in town as a result of having no virtually-stationary vehicles with their engines running."

When Brian Mawhinney announced in late 1994 that the bypass was going to go on hold, Vodafone executives were furious. The company came up with £7,500 for a fighting fund of initiatives, which they called "Newbury Bypass Now". This involved paying for accommodation and expenses of some pro-bypass campaigners and producing stickers for people to put in their cars. According to Adrian Foster-Fletcher, the Vodafone muscle was a big part of the campaign behind Mawhinney's eventual decision in July 1995 to let the road building begin early in 1996: "Vodafone certainly helped give the pro-bypass campaigners a big momentum for the road to go ahead and be built."

According to Martin Barge, writing in the magazine *Corporate Watch*, Vodafone had donated money to the pro-bypass campaign while warning employees "not to openly support the 'anti' campaign". Vodafone had also supported the Derby at Newbury racecourse: the size of the racecourse became one of what Barge believes was one of "many spurious arguments used to support the 'need' for the new road".

The nine miles of tarmac around the town, finally completed in 1998 after several years of battling between construction companies and environmental campaigners, ripped through heath, water meadows and ancient woodland. But why was Vodafone really so keen on the road? The reasons weren't immediately obvious. But as Gent took control of the company a clearer picture had begun to emerge.

The headquarters building

Gent, unlike his predecessor, had no particular affection for the large number of Vodafone buildings scattered through the town. The way the new chief executive saw it, a modern, expanding global powerhouse required a headquarters building that matched its status. Many in the town thought it disingenuous that Vodafone now cited the large number of its buildings as a reason to build a new headquarters – on green belt land just outside the town – when the proliferation of premises had been what the company had sought in the first place. One councillor puts it thus: "The Vodafone spin on the whole thing was 'oh dear, isn't it terrible, we have grown so much and we are the biggest firm in the Country or whatever, we are fantastically successful and oops we have got so many buildings, how did that happen?' But it didn't come about by accident. That was their deliberate policy."

Was there a connection between Vodafone's campaign in favour of the bypass and the desire to build its new global headquarters nearby on the green belt land? Definitely, says one senior Liberal Democrat who was on the local West Berkshire Council at the time. There was nowhere in the town centre that offered sufficient office space to match Gent's vision, but the arrival of the bypass offered new possibilities. It opened up a consider-able body of land for infill development by businesses – businesses such as Vodafone. "I think there was a link between the bypass and the head-quarters. The old A34 road going down into Newbury was very congested and the bypass road enabled them to get access to a site that they were interested in," said the councillor.

But what was this site in which Gent and his Vodafone team were so inter-ested? It was a piece of rural farmland known as the Old Showground, surrounded by other farmland, parkland, an historic house and a church. There were no other offices or industrial premises within a considerable distance of the land. This is where a somewhat curious chain of coinci-dences comes into play, which if nothing else suggests that the Conser-vative Party in Newbury and Vodafone executives were a close-knit bunch.

The Old Showground was owned by the Fairhurst family. The head of the

Fairhurst family was the late Tim Fairhurst, who among his other riches was wealthy through owning a Coca-Cola franchise in Bath. Fairhurst was what one might call a "character": he constantly quarrelled with the Council about this showground over its use for car boot sales and the number of days per year he could use it. He also had a colourful reputation in the local community and married his lover Genevieve in the last few weeks of his life.

When he died in the mid-1990s, Genevieve Fairhurst and other members of the Fairhurst family inherited a lot of money and control of the Old Showground under the Fairhurst Trust. A couple of years after her husband died, Geneveive decided to marry again. This time she chose as her husband Graeme Mather, a Conservative Member of the European Parliament (MEP). The local political connections didn't end there, with Fairhurst herself having once been the vice-chairperson of the local Conservative party.

It was well known that Whent and Gent at Vodafone were staunch Conservatives. When the land was sold directly to Vodafone for various reported amounts between £18m and £22m (figures described as "well in excess of the real amount" by Vodafone sources), some Newbury councillors cried foul.

Why were these councilors so worried? Well, Vodafone would hardly want a large piece of land just let its horses roam. Clearly if it wanted to do something with it, and with the odds heavily on building a new global headquarters in the middle of green belt land, it had to be pretty sure that it would get planning permission. To be certain, Vodafone, argued those who objected, would make good use of their contacts via the vendor Fairhurst and/or the Conservative councillors on the local West Berkshire Council.

Planning, politics and problems

There is no clear evidence that anything improper took place in the sale of the land, and Vodafone went ahead with its planning application. In November 1997 it had given West Berkshire Council its plans to build a headquarters on the Old Showground. These included seven separate buildings consisting of over 50,000 square metres of concrete slabs covering 17.1 hectares next to the new bypass. The planning department of West Berkshire Council had plenty of reasons to be hesitant about the plan. UK planning laws say that each town has an imaginary envelope around it. Inside the envelope developments are allowed: outside, they are not. The Vodafone proposal for the Old Showground was being built well outside that zone. The chief planning officer for the area, Jim Sherry, initially recommended against the Vodafone office development on several grounds, including increased traffic and housing needs. Even so, there was to be a lot of toing and froing within the Council's environmental committee before a new planning recommendation emerged. One local councillor admits: "Planning officers hated the proposal to start with as it rode a coach and horses through the regulations. But in the end, with lots and lots of pressure and lobbying from Vodafone, the final recommendation was fairly neutral – a sort of planning equivalent of the "not proven" verdict they sometimes use in Scottish trials."

Meanwhile, local politicians were itching to get involved in the debate. The West Berkshire Council was run by the Liberal Democrats and their leader, Royce Longton. Although he had supported the bypass because he was alarmed about the pollution levels in the centre of Newbury, he was against the development of a major corporate headquarters in the middle of green belt land outside the town. He was worried about the impact of the development on demand for local housing and on local transport, and the fact that a development too easily granted would make it easier for others to develop on land near to the new Vodafone headquarters. One

supporter says: "In the red, or perhaps I should say yellowy-orange, corner they had our leader Royce, a bearded ecologist who was genuinely
concerned about the impact of Vodafone on the local community and
housing in particular. In the blue corner was the former leader of the
Young Conservatives, mega-deal maker Christopher Gent. It was terribly
exciting stuff."

Also facing Longton was Suzy Kemp, the leader of the Conservative
group. A local businesswoman who had once run a recruitment and PR
agency, Kemp was strongly in favour of the development. She felt that the
economic benefits of having Vodafone based in or around Newbury were
too important to ignore.

Councillors like Longton and Kemp were initially restricted from com-
menting on the planning application while it was being discussed ahead
of the debate to give the plan full council approval. This period in most
applications for planning permission lasts for about eight weeks. In the
case of the Vodafone application, which was a complex plan attracting a
lot of local interest, it lasted about eighteen months. As Paul Walter, a local
Liberal Democrat, recalls: "It was six months from the time when
Vodafone announced its intentions to when it put in the planning application. And then it was another year while the application was doing the
rounds in the committees and so on. Vodafone faced no such restrictions
but all that time, councillors couldn't speak out and say 'well, hang on a
minute, what Vodafone has just said is not actually strictly true'."

In the absence of official political input, there was plenty of unofficial
input. On one side of the debate were Chris Gent and Vodafone and on the
other a disparate collection of environmental campaigners. As Martin
Barge of *Corporate Watch* recalls: "[Vodafone's] local face re-appeared in
the guise of a march of employees down the High Street, handing out

balloons and petitioning the Council in support of the company's application."

According to Adrian Foster-Fletcher, Friends of the Earth's Newbury coordinator and a local businessman, Vodafone encouraged its employees to write to their councillors (who couldn't comment) and tell them they wanted Vodafone to build on the new site. This campaign, says Foster-Fletcher, was incredibly effective: "I turned up at a Council meeting and the councillor said 'Mr Foster-Fletcher, yours is the only letter I've had against this proposal compared to 52 in favour'. It was a very well-orchestrated campaign – very impressive."

It wasn't just the employees who provided leverage. Foster-Fletcher continues: "Vodafone wrote to everyone whom they had helped – charities, the rugby club and so on and said 'right, you've had money from us – now you need to write to your councillors'." As sponsors of the local rugby club, one member claims Vodafone sent letters to the club suggesting that sponsorship would be withdrawn if there were no support for the planning application.

According to Foster-Fletcher, Vodafone successfully managed to pack public meetings with supporters: "I went to a lot of public meetings over the Vodafone application. At one meeting I saw ten people speaking in favour of the Vodafone project and I already knew that nine of them had a vested financial interest in so doing. One out of the ten had motivations of which I wasn't aware. At this meeting this guy I didn't know got up and declared: 'You know, I woke up early this morning and I decided Vodafone is good for the town and good for Newbury'. I suddenly thought, 'Hang on! I don't know anybody who wakes up every day and thinks that way, especially early in the morning. What's up with this guy?' A year later, I discovered that this guy's son was a senior planning officer with

Vodafone." Even local newspapers became part of the propaganda battle. The local *Newbury Weekly News* carried brochures that highlighted the role of Vodafone in the town, although the brochure did enclose voting cards asking local residents to decide whether Vodafone should stay – or move on.

On the other side of the debate, in the absence of the politicians, were Friends of the Earth and a collection of other pressure groups. Foster-Fletcher, for his part, claimed that Vodafone's proposed new HQ was awful news for Newbury's environment. "I believed passionately that it would generate traffic and increase pressure for housing in the surrounding countryside. This development was clearly at odds with Government planning policies. I argued that Vodafone should think again – and that if it didn't the Government should intervene to stop it going ahead."

There was another interest group that campaigned vigorously against the Vodafone application. The residents of Stable Court just outside Newbury had beautiful views of the magnificent Berkshire countryside. But with the Vodafone headquarters planned for the Old Showground they now faced the prospect of a series of enormous buildings blocking their view, not to mention the traffic congestion and pollution from several thousand Vodafone employees going to and from work each day. The Stable Court residents, funded by a wealthy local man, formed a small but noisy band called RAVE (Residents Against Vodafone Encroachment). Along with the Ramblers Association, Friends of the Earth, RAVE and Newbury council politicians not affected by the restrictions fought a vigorous rearguard action against the Vodafone publicity machine.

Paul Walter was disturbed by the David and Goliath balance resulting from the long enforced absence from the debate of other politicians: "Apart from the likes of Adrian, RAVE and myself, Vodafone was allowed to make all the running. The West Berkshire Liberal Democrats said that they were doubtful about the plan but that was all, there were no detailed rebuttals or anything like that."

Then there was a fear factor among many about campaigning against Vodafone. Walters says: "It's a fascinating point. It's only really if you are either retired or independently wealthy – or like me in that I've got a job quite a long way away – that you can actually oppose something locally. If you are in any business connected with the town I doubt whether you would want to put yourself through the trouble of campaigning against Vodafone. They dominate this town and if you went too far then it could affect your chances of future business with them."

The councillors were already well aware of Vodafone's dominance of Newbury. So some time earlier it had been had decided to commission a major report into the impact of Vodafone on the town and, more importantly, what would happen if Vodafone chose to leave. What the report said depends on who you talk to. Adrian Foster-Fletcher says: "The report said that it was better for Newbury if Vodafone went because you've got a small town here of twenty thousand. You've got a good position in the south of England, it's near the motorways, a lot of prosperity and we had very low unemployment even before Vodafone was here. What it said we needed was a diversified economy, not a single dominant employer."

A Conservative councillor at the time has a different spin on the report. This councillor says: "The report that came out said that if Vodafone went away the town would be no better off. I disagreed with that and thought the report was fundamentally flawed. It took little enough account of the impact of Vodafone's departure on secondary businesses, all the support businesses that had grown up because Vodafone and its employees were where they were. I think there would have been a big impact on people on employees that live here had Vodafone gone away."

The report was an embarrassment for Vodafone. They had encouraged the view that their presence in the town had a major positive commercial impact. But the report seemed to say otherwise and gave those who opposed the headquarters outright – or who just wanted to extract concessions from Vodafone before the headquarters were approved – the sort of ammunition they needed. However, Mike Caldwell, Vodafone's group corporate communications director, did a good job in limiting the damage. Adrian Foster-Fletcher recalls: "Vodafone's PR machine is mightily impressive and Caldwell has a silver tongue. He came out with a classic piece of corporate double-speak, something along the lines of 'We like this report and agree with its findings although we interpret its findings differently from others'. It helped to defuse the tension but ultimately just left everyone a bit confused as to what he meant, which I suppose was the whole idea."

The threats from Vodafone did not only exist in the imaginations of those who feared the impact that one large company can have on a community. Friends of the leader of the Council – Royce Longton, the Liberal Democrat – confirm that one day as the vote on Vodafone's application approached, Vodafone officials came in and threatened to leave Newbury altogether unless they got their way. One friend says: "They marched into the Council offices one day and said 'we want planning permission, we want that field, no other site will do and if you don't give it to us we are leaving the town. It was as blunt as that." Another friend confirms this conversation: "It was a threat, no doubt about it. They said it very nicely but it changed the whole focus of the debate. The discussion should have gone up the gears gradually as the day of the debate approached but instead it went straight from first to fifth. It just pulled the rug under all sensible debate on the subject. That's what Vodafone are like – they're bullies."

When it came to handling local politicians, Vodafone's propaganda efforts often seemed either ham-fisted or naïve. One says: "Vodafone sent around this video to all the local councillors. On it, the principal of Newbury College was saying how wonderful Vodafone was. But we all knew that Vodafone and Newbury College had close financial links and so we just laughed at it. How they thought that that sort of thing would cut any ice with us I just don't know. This was schoolboy propaganda at its worst and simply convinced the doubters that they were right to have their doubts."

A leading Conservative councillor agrees about the video, but for different reasons: "It was a classic faux pas. They sent it out registered post on the Friday. So across the area on Saturday morning, in my case at 7.30, councillors were being hauled out of bed by postmen ringing their doorbells and asking them to sign for a parcel. I thought 'oh well, at least I've got a parcel' but when I opened it all I had was this lousy Vodafone video. It wasn't what I wanted at the start of my weekend."

Sitting on the sidelines at this time was the local Liberal Democrat MP, David Rendel. Many of his constituents criticized Rendel for not coming off the fence in the debate. Rendel was widely ridiculed for stating that the issue was not a matter for a member of parliament. Critics pointed out that the fact that he was an MP in a marginal constituency might be related to his reticence. One anti-Vodafone critic says: "He was against the scheme, but thought that there would be more votes if he was in favour. Most of all, he was very keen to hang on to what he had – a seat in Parliament. He damaged the unity against the scheme by not coming out on our side." Paul Walter is more sympathetic. "I know David very well and I think that he was damned if he did say something and was damned if he didn't. Going down the middle was probably the least worst option for him. I think in his heart he would have just said 'I'm against it'. But it's utterly stupid for an MP who hadn't been involved in the discussions to make a call on that. He would have put pressure on the councillors without knowledge of the facts in what was a monumentally complex discussion."

Part of the complexity was down to the various conditions that the Liberal Democrats were seeking to attach to the proposed Vodafone move. Longton wanted Vodafone to help pay for the extra housing demands that he feared would result from the new headquarters. Vodafone had already said in advance that they would not comply with housing-related assistance. One Liberal Democrat supporter says: "The main reason we were so concerned about housing was because we thought it would create an extra three thousand jobs in Newbury when their headquarters were occupied. That's a lot of houses required and there was great pressure on land. It was difficult enough helping ordinary people to live in Newbury. We couldn't hire bus drivers or nurses because housing is just too expensive for people to afford. And we didn't ever say no to Vodafone; what we said to them was 'here is the problem. Can you help us solve it in some way?'" By "some way", the Liberal Democrats meant two million pounds to convert town centre offices into town centre housing.

Face to face

The main issue of whether Vodafone would get the go ahead for its new headquarters was to be debated by the full council and, after a preliminary debate in the Council's environmental meeting, the stage was set for a charged piece of local political theatre. The Council's usual Corn Exchange debating hall was deemed too small to house all the interested parties and so the West Berkshire Council found itself instead debating the intertwined future of Vodafone and Newbury in a large hall at the local Trinity School.

Vodafone turned up in force to the meeting with a large team of executives, lawyers and planning consultants. A local councillor says: "I was just sitting there looking at all these Vodafone suits, trying to work out how much money all these people must be being paid for Vodafone to get its way. I was still trying to work it out when, ten minutes before the meeting was due to start, Chris Gent walked in."

Gent, says the councillor, looked extremely cross –"he had a face like thunder" – and no wonder. Some of the Liberal Democrats were continuing to insist, in spite of all of Vodafone's various shades of lobbying, that Gent & Co. should cough up for the cost of local housing if the planning application was to be approved, and the vote was obviously going to be close. Gent was used to getting his way and seemed perplexed that his ambitions for a global headquarters to go with his obvious global ambition could be scuppered by a bunch of sandal-wearing lefties. His team had dramatically, many felt unnecessarily, raised the stakes of the debate by threatening to leave Newbury if Vodafone didn't get its way – and Gent was now facing the very real possibility of having to live up to his promise and relocate the business if the debate went against him.

The object of Gent's wrath was Royce Longton. But in the debate the leader of the Liberal Democrats stood his ground. "Royce made a very good speech indeed. He had all his cards there and he put the whole thing very very eloquently," said one colleague. Not being a local councillor, Gent could not speak during the debate but Kemp, the Conservative leader, made a speech which the turned one Liberal Democrat councillor's stomach: "She's a sort of sixth form school prefect type, the sort of person you grudgingly listen to. She made all the sort of points you would expect and, if you can excuse the vulgarities, her speech was several feet up Chris Gent's arse. She was talking to him during an interval in the debate and if you ask me she basically said what Gent wanted her to say."

Colleagues of Kemp not surprisingly had a different take on the speech. One says: "It's really important that it is understood that her motivations were not political at all but economic. She honestly believed that the departure of Vodafone was a serious threat to the local community." To be fair to Kemp, she was later to suffer greatly from accusations from Liberal Democrats and others that she was in league with Gent, Vodafone and the Fairhursts over the proposed new headquarters. It must be stressed that she was later cleared of any wrongdoing by an official inquiry.

The debate raged to and fro in dramatic style all evening. One councillor says: "It was one hell of a debate with quite a lot of drama. The school hall was absolutely packed and there were all sorts in there, groups of people you wouldn't normally expect to see in the same place together. There were Gent and the Vodafone top brass, the Conservatives, the Liberal Democrats and the ecological types and plenty of others too." The Vodafone people were not sitting on their hands during the debate. "They were lobbying intensely: making new offers, taking old offers away right up to the last meeting. The odds were shifting this way and that all the time and no one knew what was going to happen next."

What actually happened was a break in proceedings and this proved crucial. While the Vodafone people and their supporters talked tactics and twisted arms, the Liberal Democrats had no collective room in which to discuss tactics. Says one councillor: "I think it was mistaken on the logistics front because what we should have done is had a private room for a group meeting to discuss what had happened. There were a number of offers and counter-offers on the table and it would have been better for us to sit down and talk about what we were going to do as a group. But because we didn't Vodafone were able to pick us off one by one. I think they talked to each councillor and had carefully worked out what the bottom line of each one was."

The debate raged on, and on, and on. Every councillor had to have his say. If the rhetoric of the Vodafone entourage was to be believed, then if the proposed amendment to their planning application – the one that required them to come up with £2m for local housing – was passed Gent and his colleagues would leave their Newbury base for ever and move elsewhere. The pro-amendment Liberal Democrat believes that Vodafone's hard line intimidated some councillors: "We ended up as a divided party. We had debated it long and hard within the group many times and there was always a split between those who wanted to preserve the environment and those who were desperate to keep Vodafone for economic reasons. We had reached the decision which was that we would recommend approval on condition that they helped on the housing. And then on the night of the meeting Vodafone put a letter round everybody saying that if that was voted through they would leave. And that destroyed our unity." The Conservatives were rather more united. Although there was no official party whip that night, all their councillors supported the safe passage of Vodafone's planning application without any extra strings attached.

However, the Liberal Democrats were the largest party on the Council and even a with a modest split in their numbers, the amendment could still pass. The debate had started at 7.30 p.m., but it was not until twenty minutes before two that the crucial vote on Royce Longton's amendment to the proposal took place.

The tension was unbearable in the school hall as the results were announced. In favour of the Liberal Democrat £2m housing amendment to Vodafone's planning application there were 23 votes. Against the amendment there were – 24. Vodafone was staying in Newbury due to a solitary vote, and relieved Vodafone officials celebrated their narrow squeak.

Once euphoria among the Conservatives and Vodafone officials had died away, a second vote was quickly taken, on the Vodafone application with no extra strings attached. The Lib Dems, having lost the crucial vote but not wanting to risk losing Vodafone completely, caved in and this vote was passed by 27 to 22. Paul Walter says: "The interesting thing was that Vodafone obviously really calculated all this. I think it must have been when the seventh or eighth Liberal Democrat made a speech saying he was going to break ranks that I can remember Gent turning to someone and going 'yes, we have done it'. They had worked the whole thing out and knew just how much they had to give."

Another Liberal Democrat councillor isn't so sure that Vodafone were anything other than fortunate: "The Tories voted for it to a man or woman, though I heard later that one of them who voted for it did so with an extremely heavy heart and later retired from politics as a result. The silly thing is that you know so many small things which could have changed it; there was one Lib Dem councillor who decided to go to Denmark for a holiday instead and one who didn't bother to turn up – so many silly twists that could have pushed the result the other way. What was clear was that Vodafone were living very dangerously that night."

The following day, a clearly relieved Chris Gent said: "It was very tight and it was a great relief because we are very committed [to our new head-quarters]. We did not want to go but if they had said 'no' then we would have gone, reluctantly, but we would have gone." But would Vodafone really have left had votes not gone their way? Adrian Foster-Fletcher doesn't think so. "The bald facts were that Vodafone had no other plans to look anywhere else. They hadn't even looked beyond an industrial park site in nearby Thatcham."

Paul Walter adds: " I think the actual heart of the matter is the question of whether or not the idea of Vodafone losing was ever a real issue in the first place. There were alternative sites. They kept on going on and on about they have so many sites and isn't that terrible, even though that was their own choice in the past. It was never 'OK, if we can't have that one site at the Old Showground we'll look for two or three alternative and more acceptable sites.' They wouldn't compromise at all, which was very frustrating for everyone and very strange." Another Liberal Democrat councillor agrees: "I don't think they would have relocated had they lost the vote. I think that it would have cost them such a lot to relocate completely. And if they had they probably wouldn't have gone very far, otherwise where would they get their new workforce from? I think Gent was bluffing." If the councillor is right, then it was a massive and, many would say, reckless and unnecessary bluff for Gent to make. And if Gent was serious, then the massive cost of relocation away from Newbury would have dwarfed the Liberal Democrats' relatively modest requests for housing assistance.

There was a sting in the tail for Vodafone in this story – and rather a large one at that. Under pressure from the then Secretary of State for Transport, Environment and the Regions, John Prescott, Vodafone signed up for a green travel plan. The original number of parking spaces for the new HQ – 3,000 – had been reduced to 2,000 by West Berkshire Council. In itself this was quite limiting, but it was further pared down under the travel plan to 1,000 parking spaces. The plan was signed off by Vodafone on this basis, as the alternative would have been for the whole thing to have been blown out of the water at the last minute. This effectively meant that Vodafone had to provide a reported £10m for a green transport plan, which included providing buses and developing car share plans, to enable people to reach the site.

It wasn't all bad news on the housing front for one house in particular. One Lib Democrat says: "In the end they gave us one million pounds towards the restoration of a Grade I listed building, although they had been adamant that they would not assist on that particular issue." All other housing issues have been less satisfactorily resolved. The Liberal Democrat says: "I still have those fears about the effect of housing. And I think it will get worse when they have occupied their new HQ and the other buildings become vacant. So the worst is maybe yet to come."

Only time will tell. But if you get in a car and travel along the M4 out of London you will, after about an hour, see signposts to Newbury. South of the old motorway is the new road known as the Newbury bypass. Travel towards the town on this road and you will soon see a slip road leading off to Vodafone's new global headquarters. Look around and you will see beautiful English countryside. If you're in Vodafone's new world headquarters looking at the view, you are very lucky. If you are out in the fields looking back at this construction, perhaps you are less so.

There is little doubt that Vodafone's behaviour over its new headquarters did much to stir up resentment in Newbury. Local councillors of both parties felt that Vodafone was unnecessarily heavy handed when dealing with elected officials and planning officers. Remember what one Liberal Democrat councillor said: "To be blunt, Vodafone behaved like perfect pigs over the whole business." Up to a point, a Conservative councillor agrees: "I think Vodafone, as well, was very naive in terms of how a Council operates, how its members work. And with the benefit of hindsight they might agree with me that they didn't play it as well as they might have done in terms of understanding the democracy side of things."

In spite of his perilously close shave in the battle for Newbury, Gent was causing consternation in Vodafone's home town once again within the year. The approval of planning for the new HQ has not caused him to cease his threats. In June 2000, a government draft paper aimed at axing double-taxation relief for British-based multinational companies. Vodafone claimed that this would cost the group £500m a year, nearly half of its annual profits at the time. Chris Gent told the *Sunday Times:* "It should be in the UK's interest for multinationals to be based in the UK and not to penalize them for revenues earned overseas by double-taxing them". He added that unless the Treasury modified the draft then Vodafone would be forced to consider abandoning Britain as a base. "We have to think about our shareholders' interests," he said.

This threat also eventually amounted to nothing but, by the middle of 2000, it was clear that shareholder's minds were starting to become focused elsewhere. There were signs that the boom in technology stocks was now coming to an end. Gent's impressive achievements notwith-standing, this had helped to make Vodafone into the largest company in the UK. Gent had been looking down on the rest of the world, but the slide in stock markets was akin to a long and steep downward part of a rollercoaster ride. The following two and a half years would be the most testing of his professional life.

PART 3

A White-knuckle Ride

From Powerhouse to Penny Share

In March 2000, it seemed as though Chris Gent and Vodafone could do no wrong. On March 6 of that year Vodafone's share price touched 399 pence and it seemed only a matter of time before the stock soared up and away from the £4-a-share mark. From the time Gent became chief executive in 1997, Vodafone's stock had surged more than eightfold to this point. He had been named *Forbes* Global Businessman of the year for 1999 and was lauded by all as a brilliant dealmaker. His breathtakingly daring takeover of Mannesmann had shot Vodafone to the top of the global telecoms rankings and to the number one position in the FTSE 100. The value of Vodafone was now bigger than the previous incumbent, a distinctly old economy type of company going by the name of British Petroleum.

The story of what followed has to be the most remarkable, scary and prolonged downward rollercoaster ride in corporate history. The world economy had been growing at a steady rate since the early 1990s, with growth increasingly fuelled by investment in modern technology. In the second half of the decade a number of what most now recognize as stock market bubbles began to emerge. Growth in the stock market, if not in the real world, became increasingly reliant on the seemingly endless interest in technology, telecoms and internet stocks. The latter, in particular dot.com stocks, caught the public imagination. Suddenly it seemed as though there was an opportunity for anyone with a great idea to make money in an entirely new business medium. The business heroes of the internet were fêted as the new gold prospectors of the twenty-first century.

Now we all nod our retrospective heads and remark how obvious it was that this was an unsustainable state of affairs. Even then many were asking how it was that business success could be so easy to achieve. The media was full of stories of dot.com companies heading for stock market flotation on the back of precious little, if anything, of a track record. Spin became central to their success. Friends in the media, celebrity backers, dinner-party gossip and PR hype were routine ingredients in dot.com success. For a while it seemed as though having friends in convenient places and an effective means of getting your idea across was not so much a handy add-on to the business armoury but was rather the pillar upon which some dot.coms had been built.

By March 2000 some investors were starting to realise that the internet start-ups which failed to meet investor expectations would soon find that while business success had never been easier to achieve, sustaining it was rather more difficult. Amidst all the hype, it was becoming clear that the word "internet" was being used as an excuse for investors not to worry too much about whether a dot.com was making a profit. One could sense that the laws of gravity were about to reassert themselves as investors began to wonder where their returns were coming from.

The stock market turned frosty as internet-based businesses started to look shaky against the their old economy rivals; investors began to remember that only 10% of start-ups survive their first decade. Some internet businesses deserved their fate – they were poor ideas, badly executed – but the fallout spread to many other good businesses, including those in the telecoms sector.

Vodafone played an indirect part in spreading the malaise into the telecoms and technology sectors – and beyond. It was not only the biggest company traded on the London market, it was by far and away the most liquid, routinely accounting for more than a third of the whole day's turnover in equities. Everyone, it seems, had a view on Vodafone and Vodafone shares. Not least because there were so many shares to trade as Gent had purchased AirTouch and Mannesmann by issuing equity. By early 2003 there were 68 billion Vodafone shares in existence, while the company's annual report in 1997 stated that there were only 3 billion.

The impact of Vodafone's ailing share price was to be felt far beyond the small world of telecoms, technology and the internet. Every pension fund in the country now seemed to have Vodafone shares in its portfolio. With Vodafone, at its peak, accounting for 12% of the whole market, they had little choice. Julian Horn-Smith, the company's group chief operating officer, had admitted that executives were aware of the dependence of pension funds on a healthy Vodafone: "It is a great responsibility for Chris and for me and my colleagues sometimes, given the importance to pension funds, that we deliver." The decline in the fortunes of pension funds can, therefore, be traced in no small part to the decline of what in March 2000 was the country's leading stock. At the start of the period of decline in its shares, Vodafone was the largest company traded on the London stock market. And if Vodafone sneezed, everybody caught a cold.

The downward slope

The problem was that with so many shares on its books, Vodafone suddenly seemed to have pneumonia. On March 6, 2000, with its share price at just one penny below £4, it seemed that the company could only go from strength to strength. But as the dot.com bubble started to affect faith in telecoms and technology stocks more generally, it passed several unwanted landmarks on the long slide down. By February 19, 2001 it ceased to be the biggest stock (that honour reverted to BP) as its shares slid below £2. The last time it had been so low had been on January 1, 1999. Vodafone was not alone. European telecoms shares lost a combined £600bn over the same period. And in a humiliating moment in early May 2002, Vodafone shares moved below £1 – and for a while kept on heading downwards.

Vodafone's own problems could be traced to a number of interrelated factors. They were roughly these: that Gent (and everyone) had overestimated the growth in the market for mobile phones; that Gent (and some others, but not all) had failed to see that the £22.5bn that Vodafone and others willingly handed over to the UK Chancellor of the Exchequer, Gordon Brown, in exchange for G3 licences had in one stroke saddled a mighty company with large scale debt, with little in the way of a solid business case for even long-term returns from the outlay; and that Gent (and Gent alone) had not only ludicrously misjudged the value of his newly-acquired assets in the US and Germany, but also had little idea of how to make Vodafone businesses around the world work both individually and collectively.

For some time, it had seemed as though the demand for mobile phones would continue to rise relentlessly. But by the middle of 2000 it became clear that the steadily increasing graph of mobile phone usage was no longer a sure thing. Over the previous five years, from 1995 to 1999, sales figures for Nokia – widely regarded as the most impressive of the mobile phone manufacturers – had trebled and profits had increased fivefold. Of course stocks that always outperform the others, such as Nokia and Vodafone, will ultimately disappoint: outperformance becomes a self-defeating cycle, because one can't keep on exceeding expectations when the expectations are so high. And when Nokia announced delays to several new product launches in August 2000, its shares fell by 20% on a single day. Although the delays were put down to technical problems, it was clear that the phenomenal growth in demand for mobile technology could no longer be sustained.

Mannesmann, before it fell into Vodafone's clutches, had advocated a strategy that focused on getting the best from a combination of mobile and fixed line phones. Vodafone, however, had always placed a heavy reliance on mobile telephony. Mobiles were still selling well but it seemed less likely that the ultimate utopia of every mobile operator – that everyone would have one (or possibly more) mobile phone with fixed lines a distant memory from an earlier age – was not about to happen. Mobiles were a convenient means of contact between points, but for many people they stayed switched off once a destination had been reached. As 2000 became 2001, many wondered whether the integrated strategy might not be the more sensible one after all.

It also became clear that while Vodafone and the other mobile operators had all sort of products and services to offer the consumer, consumers weren't exactly rushing forward to try them out. With the market moving too slowly for Vodafone and others, it became important for Vodafone to change tack from selling existing services to new customers to encouraging existing customers to spend more money on new services they used – or increase what analysts called average revenue per user (ARPU). Even with the most optimistic spin, however, it was clear that ARPU figures were not going the way that Vodafone had hoped. Many users, alarmed by the expense of making calls, cut back on idle chitter-chatter and used their mobiles purely for essential calls or waited for others to ring them. ARPU was falling in many areas, squeezed by greater competition in the market and the growing number of pre-pay customers (who also spent far less than those on a contract).

Customers were beginning to use their mobiles less rather than more and certainly didn't seem particularly interested in expensive new services from what is commonly known as third generation (or 3G) mobile services. Operators like Vodafone had placed extra demands on handset manufacturers to produce 3G-compatible phones. But manufacturers couldn't see consumers beating down their doors for 3G mobile phones and didn't want to take the risk while demand seemed unproven. After all, the wireless application protocol (WAP) services provided on mobile phones had been widely ridiculed as a gimmick by consumers. So handset makers looked after themselves and cut back on the production of new handsets. This was a blow to mobile operators such as Vodafone who had gambled heavily on the rollout of 3G to consumers.

The temptation of 3G

It is easy to see how Vodafone had become excited by the commercial potential of 3G. The move to 3G potentially meant that users would be able to do many more things with their mobile phones. Phones that use 3G look similar to their predecessors but the uses to which they can be put are manifold. In the old days when all phones were fixed and none were mobile, you had to establish a direct electrical connection between your handset and the one you were calling. The same happens with current mobiles, but rather than set up a dedicated circuit a small portion of the airwaves are reserved for your call. However, this is a really inefficient way of dividing up the available airwaves because spaces and pauses in speech get the same priority as words. What 3G does is chop up conversation into dialogue packets. This means that 3G mobile networks can support many more subscribers and let them download data much faster. Your phone is also always effectively connected to the network, which means that SMS messages, emails and video clips are always available.

It was this aspect of 3G that so appealed to Vodafone and other operators.

Vodafone was willing to fight hard to get a 3G mobile licence, which the company saw being as important as the original cellular licence for which Gerry Whent had fought so vigorously back in the early 1980s. This had led to the birth of Vodafone, and now Gent and his team would part with a fortune to see a similar quantum leap in the company's potential earning power if it could get its hands on one of the licences. To ignore 3G might effectively spell commercial death for Vodafone, Gent believed, because the mobile phone would become more important than the personal computer for transmitting and receiving photos, videos, emails and the like.

Unfortunately the new Labour government, elected in 1997, had the authority over the licence process and knew it was sitting on a potential gold mine. In May 1998, the then Telecommunications Minister Barbara Roache told Parliament that the government's decision to auction 3G mobile licences would "promote and sustain competition and realise the full economic value of the spectrum to consumers, industry and the taxpayer". In the event it served only the latter, with the Chancellor of the Exchequer, Gordon Brown, gaining £22.5bn from the auction of the licences.

The bidding process was complex, gruelling and cruelly ingenious. The rules stated that the bidding must go on until there were only five bidders left – one for each of the licences available. At the centre of the bidding process was a fierce war between BT Cellnet (as it was then known) and Vodafone AirTouch for control of the largest licence, known as Licence B, which would give the winner greater capacity to exploit 3G than its rivals. These two companies were the only serious bidders for the plum licence and between them they managed to push the price up to £5.694bn. To make things even more complicated, one of the five licences was reserved for new entrants to the UK mobile telecoms market. The winner of that licence was Orange and because it was owned by Vodafone following the latter's hostile takeover over of Mannesmann, the latter knew it would have to be sold in the event of a successful bid.

Because of the way the auction was structured, with rival bids having to be a certain percentage higher, the size of the bids was escalating at an increasingly rapid rate in multiples of at least £100,000 each time. In one week the bids for Licence B rose by more than £600m in a single day. It sounds like madness and it was. The Government couldn't believe its luck. It had put a minimum price on each of the licences, which added to together made £500m, but this total was exceeded after only of a couple of bidding rounds. Analysts and experts had claimed that the firms could fork out a combined £5bn but this total too was exceeded after 70 rounds, with none of the bidders dropping out at that stage.

Ultimately there were 150 bidding rounds and bidding finally finished in April 2000, just a few weeks after Vodafone's prolonged upward surge on the stock market had come to an end. Licence A, which went to TIW, the telecoms company listed in Montreal and Atlanta and backed by Hong Kong conglomerate Hutchison Whampoa (the group who had backed Mannesmann against Vodafone), was not open to the four mobile operators in the UK. This was in order to ensure that a newcomer without an existing network could take on the current operators. Licence B, the most powerful licence available to existing mobile phone networks in the UK, went to Vodafone. The other winners of the less powerful licences – C, D and E – were BT Cellnet, Orange and One2One; they went for a little over £4bn each.

Once the bidding was over, those involved belatedly realised that they had been taking part in what, even at the peak of the technology boom, resembled an act of insanity. Losers expressed relief, while the winners became strangely coy about how they were going to make the money back. Dr Chris Doyle advised one failed bidder, the Australian Rupert Murdoch's One.Tel. Shortly after the auction closed, he pointed that out while Vodafone had a licence in its back pocket, the hole in its front pocket – to the tune of nearly £6bn – meant that it would need to generate £600 per subscriber from a subscriber base of 10 million to cover its cost. And this didn't even take into account the huge level of investment necessary to set up the network through which this was all going to happen.

Before long there were whispers that some 3G services would not roll out as quickly or be as affordable as had been promised while the race was in progress. Professor Peter Cochrane, who had been responsible for BT's 3G research program until November 2000, described the auction process as "a really good study in madness. It was a bit like lemmings going over the edge of a cliff. Some people are betting everything on this technology. If they can't find a solution, I think we will see some companies collapse." While Vodafone was in no imminent danger of this fate, it had saddled itself with debt without clear evidence that the public would want a 3G service in sufficient numbers to make the investment worthwhile. As one Vodafone sceptic remarked darkly not long after the 3G licences had been paid: "it was like Harry Houdini performing one of his famous tricks without first checking to make sure that the key was safely positioned in his mouth."

If Gent had been bold enough to risk £6bn plus development costs on 3G networks, then he and his colleagues would surely have a pretty good idea of where the return on this investment would come from. Gent was relying heavily on the idea of revenue from data services – the broader uses of a phone such as video clips, music files and so on. This is what Vodafone means when it talks about data services. Julian-Horn Smith emphasizes this when he says: "Data sounds dreadfully boring but in the digital world, everything is data." After all the very name Vodafone had been coined from combining the words VO-ice and DA-ta.

Having paid so dearly for the 3G licence in the auction, Vodafone had been keen to play up the sales proposition: that consumers would happily pay extra for data services on their mobile phones such as watching video clips of football or taking pictures and sending them to their friends. On the face of it, it seemed an attractive possibility. Mobile phone handsets with colour screens and built-in digital cameras, of the sort eventually produced by Vodafone live! in late 2002, could enable users to send rough-and-ready snapshots to each other.

Indeed, from April through to September 2000, Vodafone was already making $1.5bn, or over 5% of its revenue, from data services. The problem was that most of this revenue came from simple text messages. Although texting had meant fewer voice calls, its popularity had offered encourage-ment for the potential of the other possibilities of 3G networks.

Gent seemed very confident that the growth of e-commerce would mean a proliferation of data services. Speaking on the subject in a conference call in March 2000, as Vodafone shares peaked and the 3G licence finale approached, he said: "You will see a progressive adoption of new data services." He went on to predict that data would make up 20–25% of Vodafone's total revenue by 2004. The company had 31 million data cus-tomers worldwide who would on average spend $6.50 each. This seemed an optimistic target even back in those heady days and, when e-commerce failed to take off in the way he had anticipated, it started to look absurd. Investors, already nervous of the sluggishness of mobile sales, doubted what Gent and Vodafone were saying and continued to sell stock. By November 2001, when the market had taken a considerable turn for the worse, he told analysts: "We're about halfway there. We have lots to do."

Many thought Gent was a mite sanguine to claim to be halfway there – the share of data services from Vodafone revenue was still only 10%. Furthermore, the delay in the availability of handsets meant that by mid-2001 Vodafone had slowed the pace of development of its 3G networks, with fewer base stations constructed than had originally been planned. No handsets meant no 3G. And no 3G meant it would be silly to build a network that no one would use.

Within a few months it became obvious just how much Gent really did have to do. Essentially, he needed to come up with a Lazarus-like solution to meet his 2004 targets. In April 2002 SG Securities predicted that Gent had to produce nearly 30% of annual growth in data revenues merely to deliver overall revenue growth of 7% in the company as a whole. It was (and still is) far from clear where these future revenues were going to come from.

Sir Alan Sugar, the British entrepreneur who made his fortune in the 1980s selling Amstrad computers to a willing public, knows a thing or two about consumer demand for technology. He told some uncomfortable truths in the London *Evening Standard*: "Nobody has focused on who the hell wants this new technology. When will someone tell these people that phones are for conversation? The boom in SMS text messaging is blinding them. . . . Now it wants to deliver live video and web pages to a screen not much larger than two postage stamps. Will someone get real? The public needs to know that 3G offers a data speed only about 10% faster than a steam-driven PC."

Sugar's worries were shared by others. According to a survey carried out by the technology consultancy Detica in the middle of 2002, nearly half of all mobile phone users are unlikely to ever use their handsets for anything other than making calls. Worse for Vodafone was that more than 4 out of

10 of the population had no interest in 3G services. The worry is that services like watching clips of football matches on a mobile phone or sending photographs could prove, like WAP, little more than a fad. As one fund manager puts it: "Nobody is offering me a killer application on 3G. Nobody has yet offered me something I will pay for. My missus gets her bank statements once a week on her mobile. Quite handy. Would I pay for it? I don't think so. What is it that's so bloody attractive?"

Nevertheless, 3G supporters are not thin on the ground. Vernon de Silva, president of the privately-owned technology firm Cerebus Solutions, says: "It would be absurd to say that users don't want 3G before the applications are even available. People need to be able to use applications as part of their everyday lives before anyone can pass judgment."

It wasn't until 2002 that Gent conceded that it could take until 2005 for 3G to "really get going". One Vodafone shareholder admits: "The jury is still out on this one. But a feeling that the revenues are not coming quickly enough or in sufficient volume is causing many shareholders to assume the worst. This has certainly been a factor behind the slide in Vodafone's stock price and Gent's reputation. He wasn't alone in overestimating the importance of 3G to the present, but the fact that he has been so dogged in his belief in the 3G dream has undoubtedly been to the detriment of his personal credibility."

Criticism bites

Gent had to listen to his shareholders, especially the larger ones, but he became increasingly reluctant to listen to criticism from the media. In March 2000, he had sat atop a vast global empire, created by a frenzied year of deal making in the United States and Europe. Now he was being told by the same writers and broadcasters who had hailed him as a legendary businessman that he had made a massive blunder in paying so much for Vodafone's 3G licence. The media, having built him up for his breathtaking audacity in putting together mega deals as the stock market rose, sensed a wounded animal in Chris Gent as technology stocks went into free fall.

Before too long, journalists and analysts began to pick away at the acquisitions that Gent had already made. One of Vodafone's largest shareholders says: "Everyone knows that Gent overpaid. And as a manager he hasn't really proved that Vodafone is anything more than an investment trust and, with the current fall in share prices, not even a very good one at that." The media argument was that while Gent had proven himself to be a kleptomaniac of the highest order, did he actually know anything about running a global business?

It was, in truth, a soft target for the media. Gent had spent much of his *annus mirabilis* between early 1999 and early 2000 on the road building his global empire. He had barely sat back down in his Newbury office when critics were pointing out that Vodafone had several different brands across the world run by companies that all operated in completely different ways. Nobody knew whether Gent could knit together a consistent global business, but none of the critics could possibly tell so early on that he couldn't. In the absence of major evidence either way, these critics nevertheless began to point out difficulties and weaknesses in the various parts of the Vodafone empire as evidence that Gent, far from being a brilliant deal maker, was a reckless chancer who had massively overspent on his acquisitions at the top of a bull market.

The £100-billion-plus purchase of Mannesmann was the most obvious target. Gent had been so determined to win control of Mannesmann that he had been forced twice by Esser's stubborn fight and the movements in the stock market to move up from his original £65bn to offering over £100bn for the company. There is little doubt that Gent paid dearly for his new Mannesmann customers.

The truth is that Gent paid a very high price indeed for the privilege of running Mannesmann, even in the context of the absurdly bullish telecoms sector at that time. He certainly paid very dearly for Mannesmann's customers: effectively around £10,000 for each one. Vodafone had little prospect, even in the most optimistic of scenarios for the growth in new mobile phone customers and the spread of 3G data service, for making back that money in anything other than the very long term. Less than a year later, by comparison, Vodafone effectively spent a little over $3000 per customer in purchasing Eircom, the wireless company in Ireland.

Gent also faced massive problems persuading the Mannesmann workforce and the German general public that the Anglo-Saxon way of doing business was preferable to that favoured by most German companies. Vodafone had gone to great pains to reassure its new workforce that it would be a good employer. As soon as the acquisition of Mannesmann had been confirmed, Gent reaffirmed the assurances he had given to Mannesmann employees in an open letter of November 24, 1999. In that letter, Gent had been adamant that the takeover would not mean additional job losses and that the rights of the employees, trade unions and works councillors would be fully recognized. On February 10, 2000 Gent followed this up by meeting Mannesmann employee representatives on the supervisory board. After the meeting, the president of the IG Metall union and deputy chair of the Mannesmann supervisory board, Klaus Zwickel, declared that the employee side would now be able to accept the merger.

In truth, Zwickel could say little else, because the takeover was by that point a fait accompli. And the trade unions, though resigned to the deal, remained concerned about job losses at Mannesmann's Düsseldorf head-quarters. The conciliatory nature of Gent's meeting with Zwickel also caused problems for Vodafone back in the UK, with the Society of Telecoms Executives (STE) demanding the establishment of a relationship between the company and the union. Vodafone, which did not recognize any trade union for Vodafone staff, brusquely replied that the Mannes-mann deal had been a "special case".

The German press had been hysterical in their reaction to Vodafone's successful bid for Mannesmann. Newspapers ran headlines like "Fortress Germany falls", "twilight of the Gods for Germany Inc." and "the end of Rheinish capitalism". The *Süddeutsche Zeitung* was particularly unpleas-ant in its editorial: "Rheinish capitalism becomes more Anglo-Saxon and thus more unpleasant. Businesses will be less under the control of their supervisory boards and the banks and more directly determined by the capital market; and voices of politicians and workers' delegates will be diminished, those of fund managers and analysts amplified."

Perhaps most worrying were the complaints from German middle man-agers, not noted for their slimline administrative procedures, that the arrival of Vodafone had increased their bureaucratic workload. It is certainly a massive challenge to pull together the parts of a far-flung empire – including a sudden increase of 30,000 workers from Mannes-mann alone – without fostering a bureaucratic nightmare in the process. But as one former regional operations manager with Mannesmann said not long after the German company's acquisition by Vodafone: "The com-pany has grown like crazy. It's introducing all sorts of internal reporting requirements. Decisions take laughably long." It was clear to everyone that it would take time to align the old Mannesmann with the new Vodafone. And as Vodafone stock continued its inexorable slide down-wards, time didn't seem to be on Gent's side.

There were also problems to be picked on in the US side of the business. Gent's growth plans were based around the £43bn acquisition in early 1999 of AirTouch, whose mobile assets he had then brought into a joint venture with Bell Atlantic and GTE (themselves about to merge) called Verizon. Vodafone took a 45% minority stake, letting Bell manage the venture. As stock markets rose, this was seen by analysts as a shrewd move by Vodafone, in that it avoided at least one cross-cultural management challenge in a market of which they knew little.

Verizon Wireless is the market leader and represents 15–20% of the Vodafone group's total value. It is an important chunk of its business and, in reality, Gent was always punching far beyond his 45% stake in pushing Verizon Wireless forward. Denny Strigl, its CEO, admitted that his dealings with Gent were demanding: "Although Vodafone isn't the controlling owner of our businesses I would say Gent demonstrates controlling interest." As an example, Strigl points to Gent's insistence that Verizon introduced two-way short messaging nationwide by January 2001.

When the Vodafone share price began to falter, however, the official lack of management control became a stick with which to beat Gent. Julian-Horn Smith rejected calls for Vodafone to win a controlling interest in the venture. Of Verizon's bosses he said: "We see eye to eye on nearly every issue. There seems no need to increase our shareholding unless there is some sort of dispute or disagreement."

The "unless" was important here. In March 2001 a pretty fundamental disagreement seemed to be in the offing. The media and analysts were alarmed that Verizon and Vodafone appeared to be coming to blows over the different standards used in the US and the rest of the world for 3G technology. The two companies were at odds because the US technology –

called CDMA2000 – differed from the standard used by Vodafone's other overseas networks. Proceeding down different lines would have made worldwide connectivity nigh-on impossible in global markets. For people who wanted to use their phones on either side of the Atlantic, it was an understandable source of frustration. Duncan Warwick-Champion, head of telecoms at Standard & Poor's, the rating agency, says: "There are unanswered questions . . . particularly if Verizon does go down a different 3G technology route. What does that do for Vodafone? Can it live with it? It would look as if its global strategy comes to a bit of a halt as it crosses the Atlantic."

Verizon Wireless had been faring relatively well. By the end of 2000 it had 27.5 million subscribers – far more than any of its rivals. But a big worry for Vodafone was that Verizon Wireless was tardily making the switch from analogue to digital phones. In 2000 only just over half of Verizon's customers had digital phones, compared with 9 out of 10 AT&T Wireless customers.

The auction of new wireless licences was also a concern. Unlike most European licence sales, the US licences were sold on a local rather than a national basis, with 422 permits in total up for grabs. The process, which ended in January 2001 with 101 rounds of bidding, was only a little less tortuous than the exhausting 150 rounds that featured in the UK 3G auction. By this stage, the amount paid in the UK auctions had rung alarm bells with investors, suggesting that the telecoms companies were placing far too much reliance on the development of the 3G network, a network for which there was not yet a proven market. Consequently, the money raised in the US, at $17bn (£11.5bn), was far less than the £22.5bn paid in auctions in the UK the previous year.

In spite of growing concerns over the future of 3G, Verizon had been the most enthusiastic purchaser of the new US licences. It was the biggest individual buyer in the US auction, picking up 113 licences, more than a quarter of those available, and for these it paid \$8.8bn. Eventually Verizon was to return these 3G equivalent licences as a result of a law suit against the US government, but at the time they included two in New York City, for which it paid more than \$4m, and others in key markets such as Boston, Los Angeles and San Francisco. Never mind that Verizon was the leading player in the US market: a lack of overall management control for Vodafone, reports of rows over standardization of 3G technology, the slow conversion of customers to digital phones and Verizon's unremitting enthusiasm for new licences in the US gave Gent's critics ample firepower.

Then there was Japan and here, at least, there seemed to better news. There was no minority holding here with Vodafone now controlling the majority stake after buying out BT in 2001. Vodafone paid BT £4.8bn for its 20% stakes in Japan Telecom and the J-Phone mobile business. Vodafone chose to finance the deal through a £3.5bn placing of new shares, but with Vodafone's shares now firmly on a downward track the volume of new paper coming on to the market weighed even more heavily on Vodafone's share price.

Undeterred, Vodafone took advantage of its new control by combining the nine regional J-Phone companies into one and Julian Horn-Smith predicted with excitement: "Vodafone is the biggest foreign investor in Japan. It's fascinating how well we've been received. I am very excited."

He seemed to have good reason to be. The group drew both comfort and 20% of its revenue from its Japanese subsidiary, J-Phone. Mobile phone penetration was rising and data use via mobiles in Japan was taking off in a dramatic way, the way envisaged by Gent on a global scale. Data services such as wireless internet and picture messages were accounting for close to 20% of the subsidiary's revenues.

Others were less convinced though. One analyst warned about getting too carried away by Japan's data explosion: "Japan is illustrative, but it would be terribly naïve to assume that the success of data in Japan will be translated into success in Europe." The Japanese had social traits that just made them natural targets for a new type of mobile phone. Apart from their notorious reputation for being the most snap-happy race on earth, said the analyst, "you have to remember that people in Japan just don't talk in lifts or on trains in the way the rest of us will, so they are likely to be using data in a rather different way."

J-Phone had launched a handset that had a built-in camera (this has also now been introduced elsewhere, including the UK) and had already convinced many of its Japanese customers that it would be a good idea to switch to new handsets. Everything seemed set fair for the launch of a full 3G service in Japan, but then came another bombshell. In early 2002 J-Phone announced that it was delaying its 3G launch because of hold-ups in agreeing international standards. At the time Horn-Smith put a brave face on the decision but admitted that with so much other bad news around for Vodafone there was "a tendency for everyone to pile in and savage everything we say".

Indeed there was. Some in the media were ridiculously harsh on Vodafone as the share price kept on falling and falling. In mid-November 2001 the BBC ran articles on its website making a direct comparison between the misfortunes suffered by Gent's Vodafone and those of Marconi. The story line was that two of the UK's biggest telecommunications companies were deeply in the red. In the six months to September 2001, it reported, the two had racked up similarly large losses over the same period. In both cases, the bulk of the losses stemmed from the recent acquisitions and in both cases the two companies acknowledged that they could not hope to recover the money they had spent snapping up rivals in the earlier bull market.

Such a comparison was fair up to a point but, as the BBC belatedly pointed out itself, ultimately misleading. The difference lay in the prospects for the two companies. Vodafone had a business worth more than £100bn, with 95 million subscribers in 28 countries around the world. Marconi, however, had debts that exceeded its assets. While Vodafone carried a great deal of debt, its assets were 100 times more valuable and its sales were growing. Even so, to even have such comparisons represented a worrying state of affairs for Chris Gent. From a position of unchallenged supremacy, everything he now did was, in Horn-Smith's word, "savaged" by the media.

Perhaps the biggest kick in the teeth that Vodafone took was on May 7 when one of its own financial advisors triggered a sharp fall in its share price. Goldman Sachs – which had advised the mobile phone group on buying Mannesmann – pointed to ongoing difficulties with the German and Italian businesses. When, in the same month, Vodafone's share price slid below £1, the company had formally moved from global powerhouse to a penny share.

The Trouble with Money

Since 1997, when he took over as Vodafone chief executive, Chris Gent had hardly been a media-friendly CEO in the Richard Branson mould. Even at the top of his rollercoaster ride through his tenure, Gent's interviews were rare and interesting revelations rarer still.

Now faced with the first major challenge to his professional capabilities, Gent retreated into his shell and shunned all except the most compulsory of "opportunities" to talk to the media. As far as he became concerned, the media were out to get him, so he would therefore give them as few opportunities to muddy his reputation as possible. When he made his obligatory appearances, usually to explain massive losses due to the accounting requirement behind goodwill write downs on his acquisitions of 1999 and 2000, he increasingly came across as surly and somewhat resentful of media hostility. Worse still, he usually found himself flattened the following day by banner headlines emphasizing the former and ignoring the latter.

Although he didn't like being criticized by those whom he held in low regard, Gent could live with differences of opinion from the media on strategic matters. After all, he only had to talk to the media occasionally. Much greater damage to Gent's psyche came over the size of his pay packet, an issue that aroused hundreds of column inches of media comment, almost all of it hostile. For three consecutive years from 2000 to 2002, Gent and Lord MacLaurin, Vodafone's chairman, faced innumerable questions over the structure and justification of Gent's remuneration. MacLaurin readily admitted that the issue took its toll on Gent and some at Vodafone suggest this ultimately affected his view on how long he wanted to remain in the limelight with the company.

MacLaurin originally became chairman of Vodafone in 1998. Upon completion of the acquisition of AirTouch, however, he had stepped down to allow Sam Ginn to take over. MacLaurin assumed that that was the end of his stint in charge but when Ginn retired in 2000 he was persuaded to take the job on for a second time. Sometimes, when handling media barbs over Gent's pay, he must have wished that he hadn't.

There is no doubt that MacLaurin has had a smoothing influence on the rougher edges of the buccaneering spirit of Vodafone so beloved of Ernie Harrison, Gerry Whent and Chris Gent. MacLaurin had plenty of heavyweight experience in business. He had joined food retailer Tesco in 1959 as a management trainee and worked his way up under the wing of Tesco legend Jack "pile it high, sell it cheap" Cohen. He was on the board by his early thirties and was chairman for 12 years, during which time Tesco achieved a clear number one position in the food retailing market, before moving on to Vodafone.

Revelations and remuneration

One of Vodafone's rougher edges came in the form of a remuneration structure that appeared, to the outsider at least, to be utterly incomprehensible and overly generous. This was not a new problem for Vodafone. Both Harrison and Whent had in their time experienced major criticisms from shareholders for rewarding themselves in ample fashion for their efforts. They at least could always point to the ongoing ability of Vodafone to surpass market expectations. The same charges were now being made against Gent. He, too, had enjoyed plenty of success and had endured criticism for the same reason. But it appeared that he was being rewarded just as handsomely for the perceived failures of Vodafone between 2000 and 2002.

Controversy over Gent's levels of pay came to major public attention in early 2000, as he basked in the glory of the takeover of Mannesmann. Almost out of the blue, it seemed to critics, Gent had been awarded a £10m bonus. While many suggested that this had been awarded for successfully leading the company's hostile takeover of Mannesmann, the original intention of the remuneration committed had been to bring Gent's pay into line with his better-paid colleagues at the newly purchased AirTouch in the US.

In spite of the general euphoria within Vodafone over both deals, the size of the award was greeted with general astonishment. Vodafone management tried to sell the bonus to shareholders by making it clear that the bonus came in two parts: the first a £5m cash payment in April 2000 to bring Gent's pay into line with the company's enlarged size and the second of Vodafone shares in two years' time if the company had achieved "significant" growth in its earnings. Quite what "significant" meant was not spelled out very clearly.

Chris Baldry, the manager on voting issues for the National Association of Pension Funds (NAPF) said that his group did not approve of the bonuses because it thought the large payout did not reflect good business practices. This was essentially a transactional bonus paid for completing a takeover, albeit the largest in corporate history, when no one could yet tell whether the move represented good or bad value for money.

At the firm's annual general meeting in July 2000, MacLaurin, himself on a "modest" £480,000 salary, was heckled by investors. One heckler screamed out: "Can we have our £10 million back, please?" Raising his voice above the ensuing din, MacLaurin fell back on standard tactic that many top executives choose when losing an argument: that of "shoot the messenger". He chose not to defend the payout directly but to apologize for the fact that it had not been communicated adequately. MacLaurin told shareholders that he wanted to make an "unreserved apology" to anyone who was still unhappy with the explanations and added "with the benefit of hindsight, I believe that we might have explained it better". Gent seemed embarrassed by the fuss but stuck to the party line: "maybe our first letter to shareholders could have been better drafted," he ventured. Quite how one drafts a letter explaining away a £10m bonus in a manner that doesn't upset shareholders remained unaddressed by either MacLaurin or Gent.

In spite of the smokescreen of poor communication, MacLaurin knew he had only bought himself a brief respite from angry shareholders. The pay package was approved by shareholders, with proxy votes making up the majority of the poll. Even so 14% abstained in the vote and 15% voted against the remuneration policies of the Vodafone board. That nearly 30% of shareholders couldn't face approving the packages was symptomatic of a new phase of shareholder activism in large publicly-quoted companies. This episode, even as early as 2000, was another sign that the era in which excessive executive remuneration would go through at a sleepy AGM on the nod from institutional investors was coming to an end. MacLaurin conceded that "no such bonuses will be paid in future". Investors, alongside a media just starting to wake up to the end of the long boom in technology stocks, were watching very closely to make sure that MacLaurin kept his word.

One year on, however, and Gent faced the same debacle over his pay, albeit against a different set of circumstances. As MacLaurin had promised there were no more one-off bonuses, but this time shareholders were unhappy over the award of eight million share options earmarked for Chris Gent. Now there was also disquiet that Vodafone had paid several billion for the dubious right to have a 3G mobile licence; with a slow demand for 3G mobiles, investors seemed doubtful that the licence money would ever be recouped. In addition there were now big doubts as to whether Gent had paid too dearly for his major overseas acquisitions. Some remuneration experts calculated that it was possible, even against this background, that Gent could be in line for share options worth 23 times his base salary of over £1m, even if the company's performance was mediocre.

MacLaurin this time used a different form of wording to appease the critics. Now it seemed that the act of actually communicating Gent's pay was in good working order, but that it was easy to misunderstand what was being promised. Or in MacLaurin's words: "I do accept that the complexity of the policy allows for misinterpretation." Investors were not to be fooled, especially as Vodafone's share price had halved in the previous financial year. The mood at the annual general meeting was even uglier than twelve months earlier, when Gent and Vodafone had at least had something to celebrate. This time over 28% abstained on the question of the pay of Gent and other executives, while 11% voted against. Nearly 40% of shareholders therefore agreed that they couldn't support the board.

It is difficult to overstate how surprising it was, even a few years ago, for nearly 40% of a company's shareholders to either vote against or fail to support its executive pay schemes. A protest vote (and that is what it was) of such a size was almost unheard of, even in a climate of growing shareholder activism. The scale of the rebellion shook Vodafone's top management and this time MacLaurin agreed in public that it must review its remuneration arrangements thoroughly. MacLaurin, while defending his chief executive stoutly at the annual general meeting, also resolved in private to create a remuneration structure which was both clearly understood by all and more closely related to the performance of the Vodafone group. The company could not afford a third year of bad publicity.

However, that's exactly what it got in 2002. To be fair, Vodafone's remuneration committee – chaired by Penelope Hughes, the former head of Coca-Cola's UK arm – had been hardly been idle. It was trying to come up with a more transparent and business-aligned rewards system. Although the pay awards considered the pay of colleagues as well as of Gent himself, it was inevitably Gent who was the focus of attention. His pay deal was pored over by shareholders and the media in the most minute detail.

At its core was his basic salary: a small matter of £1.2m. Not many in the investment community were quibbling over this amount, in spite of its size. But this was just the beginning. The remuneration committee decided that Gent would be awarded share options worth seven times his basic salary (about £9m). For Gent to be able to exercise these options, he had to jump through certain hoops. Vodafone had to achieve earnings per share growth of 15% annually on top of retail price inflation. However, Gent would still get a quarter of the options with a less demanding 5% EPS a year growth target on top of RPI.

Then there were the deferred bonuses. To achieve his basic entitlement of deferred shares, worth about £1.2m, Gent was asked to beat one year growth targets based on ebitda (earnings before interest, taxation and depreciation of assets), free cash flow and average revenues per user. These targets were not disclosed, but the maximum level for the award through deferred bonuses was set at £1.8m. A separate award, which could increase the total deferred share bonus by 50%, would be achieved if Vodafone met other earnings per share targets. Finally there were performance shares, which were worth a maximum of £2.1m. To achieve this, Vodafone's share price performance had to be in the top 20% of a basket of leading global telecoms companies.

There was, however, another payment from the past hanging around like a bad smell. This was the second half of the controversial £10m bonus first mooted in 2000 following Gent's deal making "successes" with Mannesmann. Ian Jones, head of corporate governance at the Cooperative Insurance Society, said that the second half of a controversial bonus was still "a big issue" for shareholders. The media still bitterly resented the Mannesmann bonus. They saw it as a reward for deal making rather than for making the deal work, something that Gent had not yet proven beyond doubt.

It was clear that the bonus was something that had been contractually agreed. The second half was composed of shares which would materialize once further targets were met. They had been, so Gent was legally entitled to his booty even though most still regarded the Mannesmann acquisition as unproven. As Hilary Cook, director of investment strategy at Barclays Private Clients, a shareholder in Vodafone, put it: "If he met criteria set down for the bonus, he was entitled to it. There will have been an independent committee that would have decided on the bonus."

Nevertheless, others draw a parallel between Gent and Marks & Spencer chairman Luc Vandevelde, who waived his bonus in 2001 and then won new admirers as he subsequently turned the business around. Gent was clearly entitled to the money, but many believed he could and should have been more contrite about taking it.

Clearly, Gent's earlier bonus targets, whatever they were, could have been a lot tighter and in this respect the pay deal had some good things going for it. It was certainly a package that made big improvements in the clarity of what was on offer to Gent and his colleagues in the years ahead. If Gent didn't perform, he would still get a big salary by most people's standards but nowhere near the headline figures bandied around, which took his maximum possible salary as the almost certain outcome.

We will only know in the fullness of time what this complicated package is really worth, but one thing that Vodafone's remuneration committee should be given credit for is stopping the company's practice of benchmarking its pay to that achieved by US executives, where remuneration is much higher than in the rest of the world. Instead it moved to benchmark against other leading companies in Europe, even though Gent's pay ranks as loose change relative to the standards of American corporate executives. Charles R. Lee, co-chairman of Verizon Communications, the company with whom Vodafone began its Verizon Wireless joint venture, made $21m a year at the time the Gent debate was building up a head of steam.

Nevertheless, had anyone asked Gent his group's advertising slogan, "How are you?" his only possible answer would have been "I'm loaded". And because he was doing better when Vodafone was doing badly, some shareholders still saw him as fair game. In response to earlier criticism, Vodafone had consulted with investors over the pay award though the company still appeared to disregard their concerns. PIRC, the body that actively campaigns for good corporate governance, made its disquiet clear, while one leading shareholder recalled that "they consulted everywhere, but at the end of the day they are still getting paid more than last year". Another manager at a fund owning more than 1% of the Vodafone stock added: "It's out of kilter with the mood of the moment."

Others were more charitable. The influential NAPF had spoken out against the Mannesmann bonus two years earlier, but felt the overhauled remuneration system was an improvement. David Gould, the investment director at the NAPF, said: "These are old coals to start raking up. I don't think we will fight yesterday's battle." Another supporter of Vodafone's pay policy said: "We are opposed to 'fat cat' packages, but this is not one of them. The level of pay is high but it is aligned with shareholder interests." But sympathy over Gent's pay was in short supply from the unions. Jeannie Drake, deputy general secretary of the Communication Workers' Union (CWU) said: "Investors are perfectly entitled to question the company's generous bonus and remuneration schemes . . . The board also has to be mindful of the public relations consequences of continued high rewards for top managers – especially during a difficult period for the telecom sector . . . the industry has got to set an example, and while telecom workers have their belts tightened, we need to see similar commitment at the top".

The group's annual general meeting in July 2002 featured vocal opposition to Gent's pay package from several shareholders, but 84% of shareholders voted the deal through. And once the vote had been taken, Iain MacLaurin used his platform to give Gent's critics a roasting. Those that were there say it was an aggressive display by MacLaurin. He rounded on the press, accusing them of building Gent up only to knock him down. And he riled at comparisons with stricken companies such as Enron and WorldCom, calling them "odious and damaging". A few weeks later he explained his outburst to the *Independent*: "Some [of the press coverage] has been quite scandalous, almost libellous, I think."

In truth, Vodafone could hardly blame the press for poor communication when it had a reputation for being remote and unfriendly to the fourth estate. In his *Independent* interview, MacLaurin conceded the point: "I think that's fair criticism . . . maybe on the corporate affairs side of things we have got a bit behind the ball game. It that's the case we shall have to look at it. I'm talking to Chris about it. There are some very good messages from Vodafone around the world. Maybe we are not quite shouting them from the rooftops enough."

As far as most journalists were concerned, the sight of a man getting a substantial pay increase, albeit one conditional on his performance, just didn't seem right following a financial year when the company had £13.5bn in losses, the largest in corporate history. Although improvements in the remuneration structure were noted, it seemed strange that Gent's pay was so high when Vodafone's share price was now less than a quarter of its peak – back in the distant past of March 2000 – of 399 pence. Critics pointed to the actions of other European companies under pressure from shareholders following falls in their share prices. Deutsche Telekom had abruptly slashed its share options for senior managers in half. It hadn't gone unnoticed that Vodafone declined to follow suit.

In spite of all the criticism of Gent, there were few instances of investors, analysts or the media calling for his head. At the nadir of Vodafone's fortunes in early May 2002, when Vodafone shares fell through the ground to below 100p per share, Neil Ostrer, a fund manager at Marathon Asset Management, believed it was time for Gent and his board to go. He said: "I not only believe that Chris Gent should fall on his sword, I also think that some of the directors who awarded him a payment of £10 million after the Mannesmann acquisition should also resign. The Mannesmann purchase was the most value destructive in history." Other commentators stopped short of calling for Gent's head. While Vodafone's share price was performing poorly, there were plenty of basket-case companies in telecoms and technology to keep them occupied.

One of the more amusing critiques came from the British entrepreneur Sir Alan Sugar. Demonstrating a previously unexpected artistic side to his character, Sugar suggested in his regular column in the *Evening Standard* in May 2002 that at the next fund manager's meeting which Gent attended he should sing the following words (to the music of "Strangers in the Night"):

Ever since that time you made me buy everything for sight, we've done our brains in, now you're blaming me, it's really not too fair . . .
All you've ever done is cop your fee and lumber me with toot, and I'm the one to explain it all away, it's really not too fair . . .
Bankers in the plight, the gravy train's dried up and cash is very tight, and for the funds you can go away until another day;
I can tell you it's all right. I'll write it off so we can fight. We want our cash cow back and I will get it, leave me alone and simply forget the past . . .

When you find yourself serenaded by Alan Sugar, you must be in some sort of trouble. And by now Gent himself was indeed having trouble forgetting the past. The recurring issue of his pay had had a major impact on his own morale, almost certainly more than had any other criticism of his stewardship of Vodafone. As Ian MacLaurin told the *Independent* in September 2002: "I have no doubt at all that the press he has had personally has scarred him. If this sort of thing goes on he might think 'Well, I've had enough of it'." Indeed, this was a subject on which Gent himself would come to comment in the autumn days of his stewardship.

Consequences?

Gent's imminent departure seemed highly unlikely at the time of MacLaurin's comments. He still appeared to be very much in charge of what was going on. He certainly had the backing of his chairman and the support of most of his shareholders, even on the pay issue. It was no secret that Gent had already indicated that he did not intend to be running the company in five years' time and that he could leave even sooner. Sources close to the company suggested that he could leave within two to three years, but many doubted it would be that soon. In preparation, however, the question of the succession had been discreetly discussed at Vodafone's Newbury headquarters. Ian MacLaurin had signalled, after the company's annual meeting in July 2002, that he intended to devote more time with Vodafone to identify a successor. He even resigned from a job he loved – chairman of England's cricket governing body – for the purpose.

The odds seemed heavily in favour of an insider succeeding Gent. Lord MacLaurin had given little indication that he was looking anywhere else and most shareholders said that when the time came to make a change they would prefer an internal candidate. In the meantime, there was no question of Gent being forced out by an internal rival. He was known within Vodafone as a builder of strong and loyal teams. As Gent began to build Vodafone into a global powerhouse, critics of the company had pointed to a lack of the necessary depth in management quality. Vodafone had changed out of all recognition but many of the managers were the same. A senior executive of one of Vodafone's senior rivals told the *Sunday Times*: "Chris is awesome. Julian [Horn-Smith] is very, very good. People like Pete Bamford, [responsible for operations in Northern Europe, Middle East and Africa], are not in the same league. The management of the UK is no longer what it was when Chris was running it. They're living off their history. It is like the fly that was hit by the train and thought it was driving it. The business was going very well already."

Julian Horn-Smith (who had been promoted to group chief operating officer for the company) already had a very deep understanding of what was going on in the various areas of the organization. If Gent went sooner rather than later, it seemed almost a certainty that he would be the successor. Popular with colleagues, he already ran the company on a day-to-day basis as Gent concentrated on wider strategic issues. Horn-Smith's role was almost overlooked in the all the hullabaloo surrounding Vodafone's bids for global supremacy with AirTouch in America, Mannesmann in Germany and J-Phone in Japan. His disadvantage was his age: he was roughly the same age as Gent, being only seven months younger. Horn-Smith himself said that he was not interested in thinking about the leadership, adding ironically (as it turned out): "He's not about to go tomorrow and he and I are close personal and business friends."

As he made acquisitions across the world, however, Gent had been very smart in getting other leadership candidates into his team. Gent's other likely successors were not British and their appointment could have caused a stir. Vittorio Colao is an Italian in his early forties, who is responsible for the group's Southern European operations and came to notice when he was appointed to the board in April 2002. Colao used to be a McKinsey consultant and was closely involved in the creation of Omnitel, Italy's number two mobile operator which was subsequently bought up by Vodafone. The other potential leader was fellow board member Thomas Geitner. In his late forties, the German is responsible for the group's products and services. His popularity at the Newbury headquarters is very high because of his thoroughness and attention to detail in leading the development of the recently launched Vodafone live! mobile service.

Yet even in November 2002 it seemed that Gent would stay put for some time and that his internal heirs apparent would have to wait. MacLaurin had noted: "He could go and work in America tomorrow and earn ten times what he's earning here." That seemed unlikely: Gent was the archetypal Englishman and seemed destined to stay put. However, the reverse logic was also pointed out by a Vodafone colleague: "Privately, Chris is fed up with the discussion of his pay. If he were to leave . . . [a successor] would have to be found in the US, which would be more expensive." A prescient comment if ever there was one, given the eventual choice of his successor.

PART 4

Stepping Off the Rollercoaster

Back in
Fashion

With doubts about its performance, the future of 3G technology, a limp share price and three years' worth of criticism of Chris Gent's pay package, the bottom of Vodafone's rollercoaster ride had been reached. By the summer of 2002, Vodafone's share price had been falling almost continuously for well over two years. The group for a short while was valued at less than a quarter of its peak of 399 pence per share way back in March 2000. How long ago the glory days now seemed.

Yet even at this moment, any rational analysis of Vodafone's balance sheet told a different story. When Vodafone announced its latest figures in May 2002, it reported pre-tax losses of £13.5bn – equating to £37m a day. Yet its share price flickered into life. The figures had not been nearly as bad as had been expected. To Gent's obvious dismay, the focus of the media on his pay and massive headline losses had obscured strong cash flow and low debt relative to Vodafone's competitors.

There was also lots of other unreported good news. Vodafone had more than £6bn in the bank to spend. It could have used the money to make shareholders feel better by buying back some of the huge number of shares it had issued in the course of its various acquisitions, but decided against doing this. The company also resisted calls to raise its dividend in order to push its flagging share price back up. One person familiar with the Gent's thinking told the *Observer*: "They've increased the dividend for the past 13 years, but you have to temper expectations with the fact that Vodafone is a business which has made it quite clear that it will invest in third-generation technology in terms of building capacity as well as adding products and services. That involves heavy capital spending. In addition, acquisition opportunities might present themselves over the coming months. You cannot do that and hike the rate of the dividend." Vodafone was also still in the market for cut-price acquisitions and bought up extra shares in Cegetel, owner of the French mobile operator SFR and currently controlled by Vivendi.

Over the months that followed there wasn't any more particularly good news to report. In fact, there didn't seem to be any news at all. Vodafone, noted analysts, even by its own uncommunicative standards, had gone decidedly coy over the company's performance in the first half of the fiscal year 2002/3. Real or imagined, it seemed as though Vodafone had adopted the corporate equivalent of "radio silence". As the day that Vodafone was due to announce its results drew near, experts, commentators, analysts and investors made their forecasts on the basis of scant information.

When the day arrived it was clear that this had been a deliberate act: Gent was now in a position to thumb his nose at his critics. So it was that on November 12, 2002, Gent found himself at that press conference in the Savoy Ballroom announcing spectacularly good half-year figures to an astonished array of investors, analysts and journalists. Turnover had increased by two-thirds benefiting from the inclusion of results from the group's Japanese operations, with new data revenues, Vodafone's great hope for the future, rising sharply in that region. Profit before tax and before goodwill increased by over 40%, while earnings per share increased by over 30%. Money was still being spent on investment in building 3G capacity, cash flow was strong at nearly £3bn and net debt was on a clear downward track.

Of particular note was the achievement of in the profit margin of J-Phone, up from over 20% in the previous year to 32% in this. And as well as the cash for an extra stake in Cegetel, it was revealed that Vodafone had enough left to complete the buyout of remaining minority shareholders in the old Mannesmann, now Vodafone AG, in Germany.

Julian Horn-Smith, announcing the nitty-gritty of the results that day, was clearly overjoyed. "I'm personally delighted by this set of results. All around the world our brand is becoming better used and more widely known. Vodafone is simply getting stronger and stronger. Key operating measures are doing better than expected. Strong brand and service offerings have given Vodafone a unique place in the market. This gives us a compelling vision of the future."

You would expect a group chief operating officer to put a positive gloss on any set of results, excellent or not. Yet Horn-Smith's words, after two and a half years of cynicism, suddenly seemed more believable. Underneath the headlines, the sub-plots all seemed to be equally encouraging. In spite of already high levels of penetration in many markets, Vodafone had achieved an increase in organic growth of 10% in the year to September 2002, with a growth rate of nearly 30% in Asia, Italy and the United States. The customer mix had improved markedly, particularly in the United Kingdom and Germany, with a sharp rise in the more lucrative contract customers versus prepaid customers.

In a move that offered great encouragement for the launch of the first 3G network in Japan at the end of 2002, J-Phone had also taken a disproportionately large share in the market share of camera phones. This boded well for the growth of camera phones elsewhere, including the launch of Vodafone live! services. More than half of Vodafone customers in Japan now had such a phone. The combination of data services growth combined with versatile handsets had pushed the percentage of not-voice growth in Japan over 20% of the total for the first time.

Vodafone live! and Vodafone office, said Horn-Smith, would now increase the successful Japanese camera phone strategy overseas. Horn-Smith said that both should start to have an impact in the second half of 2004. And Gent added: "We're banking on new data and hence growth environment, because we're convinced of long-term growth prospects."

Verizon Wireless now also seemed to be coming along nicely. It had been asserting its market leadership with about 1.5 million extra customers in the first half of 2002/3. AT&T had achieved less than half that number, and Cingular and Sprint were lagging well behind. On the crucial question of ARPU, Vodafone executives were adamant that it was on the rise, with total contract minutes used per customer growing steadily. And Vodafone's sponsorship deals with the likes of Manchester United and Ferrari, together with the consequent development of a global branding campaign, were yielding economies of scale on marketing across the board.

The presentations over, Gent prepared to take questions. What would investors, analysts and the media make of it all? The first, about possible network problems for camera phones, was dismissed by a violent shake of the head from Gent, followed by a brief lecture to his questioner. Next came the inevitable question about the large write downs on assets. "We will have to write down £13 million each year for the rest of this decade; it's an accounting obligation," was the response. After another couple of questions several other people had their hands in the air, but Gent, whether because the stage lights were bright or because he preferred not to see them, said quickly: "No more questions? OK, thank you all for coming. I think you'll agree that . . ." Suddenly, a voice from the Vodafone side of the stage shouted "Erm, Chris, I think there are some more". Gent looked up, squinted into the darkness ahead of him and moved back into rapid combat mode.

What will distinguish Vodafone live! from Orange's equivalent product? "Go and ask the users." When will G3 create returns? "When we're happy that it's reliable and there are enough of the right handsets around – the middle of next year. In Europe we're six months behind Japan." How much longer will you hang on in the US? "Look, I know you journalists live in a half-empty world, but the fact is that US results look good in their local currency." When Hutchison comes to the UK market, will you be able to match their low tariffs? "There's nothing that they can offer that we can't offer." Who will make the 3G handsets? "Premature to talk about that. The usual suspects."

Time for one more. The corner, it seemed, had been well and truly turned; it was a classic performance by Gent, full of encouragement for the future and the inevitable sideswipes at the media. Then I asked Gent the final question, as I described at the start of this book.

Question: There have been recent rumours about long succession planning for your position within Vodafone. But do you, given these results, now plan to go on and on and on?

Answer: [laughs] I've always made it clear that that's not the case. I'm a steward of the company rather than a permanent incumbent, BUT [emphasizes word] there's plenty of things to do with this business. It's performing extremely well and I'm having a great time. Given that we're making a lot of progress on impor-

tant initiatives, I don't think that you'll see me out of the door quite as quickly as maybe you hope [suddenly quickens pace of delivery]. Just to say, succession planning is an important issue . . . and I'm sure that the main board will have in mind what it thinks it needs to do on the timescales I've discussed with them about the future. There's plenty to do in this business, it's really going places."

After this, the music suddenly started again. The lights went up and the press conference was over. The journalists scurried away to write their stories. And there was only one story they could be writing that day.

After the show

It was not surprising that the results of Vodafone were being watched quite so closely by the media. It is almost always the most heavily traded stock in London and has the biggest impact on the movement of the FTSE 100. On November 12, one day's turnover in Vodafone shares matched the market capitalization of a middle ranking company and was responsible for half of the FTSE 100's increase. By the end of the day more than one billion Vodafone shares had changed hands through the stock exchange's automatic dealing system, a third of the total number of shares dealt in the UK and one of the heaviest daily volumes in the stock in 2002. Most significantly of all, turnover saw Vodafone return from the land of the penny share. Prices rose from 98.5 pence per share to above 111 pence by the end of the day. For investors, Chris Gent and Vodafone were suddenly back in fashion. The media reaction was equally unambiguous.

The Times ran a headline "Vodafone turns the table on its critics". Writing in the paper's Tempus column, Robert Cole noted: "Investors, it is well known, are prone to mood swings. They are liable to get wildly overenthusiastic on the way up and are also likely to get overly dejected when things go awry. But the notion that was doing the rounds earlier this year always seemed to suggest that investors were allowing their depressive tendencies to get the better of them. Yesterday's interim results from Vodafone presented evidence that the mobile telecoms industry is a long way from going ex-growth."

The media too had been prone to large mood swings. For the previous two and a half years, it had been fashionable to knock Vodafone and everything it did. But even the Vodafone share slide story had become boring for the media to write about. And over at its sister paper the *Sunday Times*, the rare sound of journalists eating humble pie was distinctly audible. The then Agenda columnist, Rory Godson, referred to criticism from the pages of his own newspaper a year or so earlier, that while Gent was good at buying businesses, he was less good at running them. Godson praised the latest Vodafone figures and conceded: "Because the £100 billion takeover of Mannesmann puts nearly all other deals in the shade, it is sometimes easy to forget that the Vodafone army never sleeps. Over the past two years, Gent has been investing billion upon billion to take control of big businesses in Japan, Spain, Ireland and elsewhere. Yet the operational performance has rarely faltered . . . Vodafone entered the telecoms downturn in a position of almost unchallengeable strength. Orange, T-Mobile, mmO$_2$, all its would-be rivals are hampered by a combination of debt-encumbered parents, loss-making businesses or patchy geographical coverage."

That outsiders had been kept in the dark prior to the release of so much good news was not forgotten. Newspapers wasted little time pointing out that Gent's revenge on analysts had been sweet. Neil Collins, the City Editor of the *Daily Telegraph*, ran the headline on his City Comment column as "Text message to the boffins: you were just so out of the picture" and followed up with: "Well, that'll show 'em. Vodafone must be one of the most heavily analysed businesses in the world and yesterday it became clear that the ranks of experts had hardly a clue how it has been doing. The results are so much better than their expectations that there were mutterings about the company wanting to teach them a lesson in return for all those months of market misery. . . . Vodafone's current advertising campaign asks 'How are you?' To which the City's boffins can only reply: 'Completely wrong-footed, thanks'."

The boffins themselves didn't seem that put out by their misjudgments. John Tysoe, an analyst at WestLB said: "They have beaten all the forecasts. This has been helped by the growth in the customer numbers. On a like-for-like basis, revenues have grown by 15% and the synergies from its acquisitions are beginning to take effect." One of the biggest objectors to Gent's pay package had been Tim Rees, head of investment at HBOS's Insight Investment. He acknowledged that Vodafone had achieved a "very impressive set of results", although he was still concerned about the way in which Vodafone carried out corporate governance. Another analyst told the *Financial Times*: "Vodafone has drawn a line in the sand. Cash flow is so strong that it has the flexibility to decide what to do in going forward, regardless of the state of the rest of the industry. It now looks likely to roll out 3G infrastructure ahead of the competition." Simon Weeden at Goldman Sachs agreed that the results "not only showed strong profit improvement but also that Vodafone . . . can deliver revenue growth".

At least one other analyst noted however that Vodafone had much to prove. Mustapha Omar, at Collins Steward, said: "The launch of [rival] Hutchison in the UK will squeeze margins and the regulator will curb roaming charges." Another dissenter said the figures reflected a "better execution by the management, rather than the mobile phone sector regaining its growth". John Karidis, analyst at Commerzbank agreed, saying: "These are excellent results, but on the back of reasons that are not sustainable. They are largely driven by margin improvement rather than revenue growth . . . Vodafone's performance looks very vulnerable to regulatory attack and we have yet to see what new entrant Hutchison 3G has up its sleeve. Its arrival could herald a wave of tough competition in mobile tariffs."

What challenges now awaited Vodafone? According to Rory Godson of the *Sunday Times*, the threat was not from within Britain. "[There is not] much prospect of a challenge from America, because of that market's fragmentation and early maturity. The long term threat is more likely to emerge from China or Japan." Referring to Vodafone's relentless push for other acquisitions, Godson noted Gent's new confidence: "Gent does not seem unduly bothered. He seems to know that he will win in the end."

Perhaps because he knew how to judge when the end had arrived.

10 Now You See Him, Now You Don't

When John Major, Chris Gent's friend from his early days back in South London, lost the general election of 1997 he knew that there was no sense in carrying on. The former Prime Minister left Downing Street with the words "when the curtain falls it is time to get off the stage, and that I propose to do".

In truth, Major's decision wasn't a difficult one; his curtain had been falling for some time. But when Gent announced on December 18, 2002 that he was to step down as Chief Executive of Vodafone in July 2003, there was genuine astonishment. It had been well known that Gent didn't plan to go on indefinitely. Plans to find his successor were developing, but almost everyone believed that this meant two or three years down the road. Gent had endured a rollercoaster ride of fortune over the previous six years at the helm of Vodafone. And having just delivered a startlingly good set of results it didn't seem as though his curtain was about to come down any time soon. Indeed most reckoned that the second act of his play had barely begun.

Yet a few weeks after his barnstorming performance in November 2002, Gent dropped his bombshell. He had made the decision to step down at the end of July 2003. Furthermore, his successor had already been found.

Into Gent's shoes will step Arun Sarin. Although little known in the UK, Sarin, the son of a lieutenant-colonel in the Indian Army, has a formidable reputation in the mobile phone industry. His career path has criss-crossed with Vodafone on several occasions. He was heavily involved in Mannesmann's bid for a mobile licence in Germany and as chief executive of AirTouch International prior to its merger with Vodafone. After the merger, he was given a place on the Vodafone board and spoken of as a potential successor to Gent. But when Gent merged the American business with that of Bell Atlantic and GTE to create Verizon Wireless, he couldn't find a role big enough to keep Sarin happy. Sarin went off to run two smaller firms in California but, but now he was back – this time as Gent's successor.

Why did Gent decide to go? His attitude to his future, as has been shown, suggested that his departure was not imminent. Gent was never going to tell the truth about when he would depart, especially not in front of the world's media. But the fact remains: no sooner was Chris Gent back in fashion, than he was gone. And yet there are no particularly dark reasons for Gent's departure: no secret putsch, no dirty dealings, no sense of a CEO falling on his sword or jumping before he was pushed. Instead, it seems that Gent had just simply had enough.

Personal issues are an important consideration here. Gent is in his mid-fifties, but has a young family from his second marriage. His children from his first marriage grew up while Gent was busy working his way up the ranks. Doubtless Gent will find time for other commercial and leisure activities, but when he says he wants to retire to spend more time with his family it is likely that, unlike most current or former politicians, he is telling the truth.

Gent has remarked in the past that when he left Vodafone, he wanted people to wonder "why now?" rather than "why did he hang around too long?" The smartest people are those who leave their audience wanting more. The peaks for which Gent will be remembered, as he sat atop the mobile telecoms world at the helm of Britain's largest company following a year of astonishing deal making in early 2000, were unlikely to return. But Gent was sufficiently smart to know that if you can choose when you go, you can go when you are at least back on the up. With the impressive results he delivered in November 2002, and having totally wrongfooted his critics, Gent perhaps decided that the criticism on everything he did or said had been weathered and that now was his moment to step off the rollercoaster.

The most serious damage to Gent's own psyche probably came over the size of his pay packet rather than over any other issue concerning his stewardship. Gent has always been notoriously sensitive to press criticism. As we have seen, Ian MacLaurin has readily admitted that the issue took its toll on Gent and may have affected his view on how long he wanted to remain in the limelight. Gent himself eventually admitted as much publicly at a dinner in his honour in Cannes in February 2003. He described his huge pay package as his greatest regret and "a bridge too far". He also said that he wished he had told the Vodafone remuneration committee that the package was too big. It was a stunning *mea culpa* from a man not known for admitting his mistakes publicly, yet the fact remains that ultimately he did nothing at the time to stop the controversial pay packages from going through.

It is not too early to say something about Sir Christopher Gent's legacy for Vodafone. Instant obituaries on his stewardship described him as the man who made Vodafone, but Gent himself would probably point out that for fifteen years before he took over as chief executive, Vodafone was energetically driven by the combined talents of Ernest Harrison and Gerry

Whent. With their swashbuckling entrepreneurial spirit they took Vodafone from a small offshoot of Racal, gambling on unproven technology, into the forefront of UK mobile telephony. Gent was the managing director of Vodafone for much of this time and owes a great debt to Whent in particular for the entrepreneurial skills he developed during his "apprenticeship" for the big job.

When his opportunity came, however, Gent was a revelation. Although he impressed many with his sure handling of Vodafone's internal affairs in the early years of his stewardship of the company, his eye was always on opportunities for international expansion. The group was top dog in the UK. It had dallied in some ventures in Europe, but lacked a strong presence there. It had interests in Asia but could do better and it had nothing to speak of at all in North America. Gent was already looking for the big one.

He found it by merging with AirTouch in the US. A few months later, he mustered an amazing diplomatic coup in persuading Bell Atlantic, the company he had beaten off in his pursuit of AirTouch, to throw their lot in with him in a joint mobile venture that stretched across the United States. Then only a few months later Gent, enraged by the German telecoms giant Mannesmann's audacious swoop for his UK rival, Orange, responded with an audacious swoop of his own – for Mannesmann. The machinations between Gent and Esser, Germany's arcane takeover laws and the hostility of the German media and politicians made the takeover a minefield – and certainly one of the most dramatic and exciting ever seen, especially when it finally emerged that Mannesmann had a £100bn price tag attached to it.

Gent fully deserves his reputation as a brilliant dealmaker for these moments alone. But what this book has not been able to show, in the interests of clarity, are the innumerable smaller deals in which he has been involved around the world: an increase in a minority stake here, a quiet little takeover there. While everyone has been talking about the "big bucks" deals, it has been the regular flow of "little bucks" deals in many other countries which have helped just as much in establishing the reputation of Vodafone as a major global player.

When the technology bubble burst and reasons were sought for Vodafone's share price weakness, critics began to suggest that Gent was a deal maker at heart, but not the right man to knit together a consistent global business. And worse still that Gent, far from being a brilliant deal maker was a reckless chancer who had massively overspent on his acquisitions at the top of a bull market. At that point nobody yet knew whether Gent could run a coherent global business, but none of the critics could possibly tell so early on that he could not. As for overpaying: yes, the values Gent paid look staggeringly high with the benefit of two years of hindsight, but they were not out of line with the crazy world of telecoms mergers and acquisitions of 1999 and 2000.

Many with only a casual acquaintance with the business world are curious as to why Gent and Vodafone have been able to go on spending on acquisitions in the years when the share price has been on a massive downward slide. Vodafone's share price has certainly suffered for a number of reasons, but that is to confuse the fortunes of equity with debt. Gent's smartest move has been to finance his major acquisitions through issuing equity rather than borrowing. That's a lot of equity to issue: as we have seen, the 1997 annual report, at the start of Gent's tenure, claimed that there were 3 billion shares in circulation; now, thanks to the equity purchase strategy, there are 68 billion.

The result has been that Vodafone shares have been as common as snowflakes at the North Pole. This has been bad news for those looking for a quick buck in a bear market, but not such bad news for the long-term future of the company. And it is also worth noting that in spite of Vodafone's long slide in share price, it remains among the top twenty of the largest companies in the world. Vodafone's lack of debt, at least relative to its major competitors, combined with an excellent flow of cash coming in from its newly acquired businesses around the world has put it in a very strong position for the future.

This has been just as well, because it is not clear that the billions that Gent and Vodafone paid out for its 3G licence in the UK will give Vodafone a return any time soon. The 3G licence auctions of 2000, at the height of the boom in technology stocks, will go down in history as a really good study of collective madness. Ever more ridiculous sums of money were offered over the course of 150 exhausting rounds of bidding over several months. And once the bidding was over, losers expressed relief while the winners worried about how they were going to make the money back. Vodafone has unambiguously thrown its future behind the growth of data services, by which it means picture messaging, SMS text, video clips and so on; all things that will mean that customers will have more reasons to use a mobile phone.

All Gent had done, said critics, was to go on a buying spree for a 3G technology that people simply didn't want. Widespread 3G services are certainly some way away and when they do come they will not deliver results in big enough numbers to live up to expectations. In a October 2002 report the research group Forrester suggests that expectations from 3G licence holders are still hopelessly optimistic. The report indicates that 3G licence holders would have to triple their number of users to break even within the next five years. A more likely scenario, it says, would be for a profit from 3G by 2014, seven years later than hoped. And it also suggests that only 10% of mobile users would use the new technology by 2007, a fifth of the figure projected by the mobile operators themselves.

Vodafone's Japanese operations suggest that Forrester, once lampooned for being too sanguine on every issue concerning technology in business may now be erring the other way. Camera handsets are selling heavily and Vodafone has now launched the first 3G only network there to support the development of the mobile phone as more than just something to talk into. It will be a few years before we see whether the rest of the world is as thrilled with 3G as the Japanese may yet become.

While it is too soon to call Gent's foray into 3G a blunder, the intentions behind his determination to beat others to a licence is understandable. After all, when bidding for the original cellular licence that made Vodafone's name, Gent's predecessor Gerry Whent had spent big money on unproven technology. He knew that you couldn't make money without taking chances and being brave. Brave because that also involved huge investment in infrastructure, the placing of antennae all over the country and systems to charge those using the system. Gent has similarly had to invest large amounts of money in building Vodafone's 3G network. In this sense, he has at least admirably maintained this buccaneering spirit within Vodafone. And at the end of the day Vodafone has the 3G licence and if it repays its cost, its rivals will be nowhere.

It's fair to say that over the period of his tenure Gent probably occasionally did take reckless and unnecessary chances. The silliest was perhaps in his own backyard of Newbury, where he managed to turn the molehill of a proposed relocation of staff into a massive mountain of bad press about a large corporation bullying its local community in order to get its way. Gent and his team seemed to treat the issue like a hard ball session of negotiation with another corporate giant rather than a small local council.

Vodafone's clumsy efforts left it embarrassingly close to being forced to undertake a massively costly relocation elsewhere.

Although its image suffered greatly at home, the same could not be said for Vodafone's image abroad. When Vodafone made its series of acquisitions many of the newly acquired customers seemed unfamiliar with the Vodafone brand. Europe in particular was a branding nightmare: a company with a whole bunch of other companies across the continent, each with a different brand name. In Germany, Vodafone was Mannesmann; in Italy, Omnitel; in France, SFR; in Spain, Airtel – and so on through many other European countries. Even its identity in the UK had been confused by changing its name from Vodafone to Vodafone AirTouch and back again. The company needed to generate a global brand to make the most of its global power. Gent and his team chose to do this through the sexiest sponsorship deals possible. Critics moaned that they threw away money on advertising, yet had it not been spent the group would remain a powerful but anonymous holding name for a disparate bunch of interests dotted around the world.

Finally there was the legacy for which Gent, perhaps a little unfairly, will perhaps be most remembered by the man in the street. By international standards, Chris Gent's pay was not extreme for the chief executive of a multinational company. But the way in which his pay became the subject of countless column inches of newspaper analysis cannot be mainly be the fault of an intrusive media. Three years running, the issue raised controversy not only in the press but at the company's own annual general meetings. In 2000, the controversy came over a £10m bonus for acquisitions that hadn't yet proved their worth. In 2001, it was about millions of share options granted without a clear explanation. By 2002, Gent's rewards, though still potentially staggering, were becoming more closely linked to his performance. But the damage to Gent's reputation and to the corporate governance capabilities of Vodafone's remuneration committee had already been done. As far as most journalists were concerned, the issue was more one of contrition: by May 2002, the sight of a man accepting a substantial pay increase, albeit one conditional on his performance, just didn't seem right when set against a year when the company had £13.5bn in losses, the largest in corporate history, and when the share price of Vodafone was less than a quarter of its peak.

Overall, what Gent has achieved in six years as a chief executive of Vodafone has been little short of astonishing. Perhaps the best measure of his achievements is to ask what would have happened to Vodafone had he not been so daring in acquisitions, be they of companies or licences, or so bold to choose the likes of Manchester United and Ferrari as sponsorship targets. Had it remained a predominantly UK mobile player, Vodafone would have been doomed long since. Other operators, owned by bigger brothers in France and Germany, would have been better placed to provide international networks to business customers.

The agenda that Sarin encounters will not amount to this sort of "expand or die" dilemma. He will face a different series of challenges. It seems unlikely that he will encourage Vodafone into a repeat of the mega deals that characterized the Gent years. He will therefore have a big opportunity to run the business more conventionally, with higher dividends for shareholders and possibly share buybacks. A much higher priority will be placed on getting as early a return on Vodafone's 3G mobile licences as possible. That threatens to be a long haul. Then there is the question of Vodafone's minority stake in Verizon Wireless. Sarin knows the US market very well and may decide that a majority stake is required for Vodafone to get the most from its acquisition. He will also need to make sure that the group's cohesion moves well beyond sexy sponsorship deals and a common global brand. And given that his leadership rivals included internal candidates he is going to have to find a way of making the most of the talents of an in-house team deeply loyal to Gent and wary of what the new chief executive will bring to the party.

However, those issues are for the future. The legacy of Chris Gent is that he changed Vodafone out of all recognition from mid-sized player to global powerhouse in the midst of a frenzy of acquisitions in a crazy bull market. Dan Roberts of the *Financial Times* put it well when he wrote of Gent: "A mixture of stubbornness, charm and good timing was vital to his year of deal-making; stubbornness to try what everyone else said was impossible; charm to persuade the investment community to keep on writing him blank cheques; and the timing – or luck – to buy with shares when the bubble burst." Gent then endured withering criticism on several fronts, in particular for paying over the odds for his acquisitions, his judgments on 3G technology and, in particular, his salary.

In the end he was able to stick a resounding two fingers up to the world and step off the rollercoaster at a moment of his choosing. And once he's gone, life will seem a little duller.

Index